Exploring
Numerology

Life by the Numbers

By

Shirley Blackwell Lawrence, Msc.D.

NEW PAGE BOOKS
A division of The Career Press, Inc.
Franklin Lakes, NJ

EXPLORING NUMEROLOGY
EDITED AND TYPESET BY NICOLE DEFELICE
Cover design by Mada Design, Inc / NYC
Printed in the U.S.A. by Book-mart Press

To order this title, please call toll-free 1-800-CAREER-1 (NJ and Canada: 201-
848-0310) to order using VISA or MasterCard, or for further information on
books from Career Press.

The Career Press, Inc., 3 Tice Road, PO Box 687,
Franklin Lakes, NJ 07417
www.careerpress.com
www.newpagebooks.com

Library of Congress Cataloging-in-Publication Data

Lawrence, Shirley Blackwell.
    Exploring numerology : life by the numbers / by Shirley Lawrence.
        p. cm.
    Includes bibliographical references and index.
    ISBN 1-56414-651-0 (pbk.)
        1. Numerology. I. Title.

BF1729.N85 L343 2003
133.3'35—dc21

2002041095

The Keys to My Personal Numerology Chart

Name _____ Birth Date _____

I. Soul's Urge/Desire (vowels) _____

II. Mind/Personality (consonants) _____

III. Total Expression/Destiny (vowels and consonants) _____

IV. Inner Guidance (root of full name number doubled) _____

V. Birth Path (root of your birth month, day, and year) _____

VI. Golden Goal (root of Total Expression
plus Birth Path) _____

VII. Karmic Lessons (Numbers missing in the name) _____

VIII. Planes of Expression:

Physical Letters _____ Number of letters _____

Mental Letters _____ Number of letters _____

Emotional Letters_____ Number of letters _____

Physical Letters _____ Number of letters _____

IX. Challenges and Opportunities

1st Challenge _____ Birth to Age _____ 1st Opportunities _____

2nd Challenge _____ Age _____ to _____ 2nd Opportunities _____

3rd Challenge _____ Age _____ to _____ 3rd Opportunities _____

4th Challenge _____ Age _____ to _____ 4th Opportunities _____

The Keys to My Personal Numerology Chart

Name (with a W) _____   _____

I. Soul's Urge/Desire (vowels) _____   2nd Desire (W as a vowel) _____

II. Mind/Personality (consonants)_____   2nd Desire (W as a vowel) _____

III. Total Expression/Destiny (vowels and consonants)   _____

IV. Inner Guidance (root of full name number doubled)   _____

V. Birth Path (root of your birth month, day, and year)   _____

VI. Golden Goal (root of Total Expression plus Birth Path)   _____

VII. Karmic Lessons (Numbers missing in the name)   _____

VIII. Planes of Expression

Physical Letters _____   Number of letters   _____

Mental Letters _____   Number of letters   _____

Emotional Letters _____   Number of letters   _____

Physical Letters _____   Number of letters   _____

IX. Challenges and Opportunities

1st Challenge ____ Birth to Age ____ 1st Opportunities ____

2nd Challenge ____ Age ____ to ____ 2nd Opportunities ____

3rd Challenge ____ Age ____ to ____ 3rd Opportunities ____

4th Challenge ____ Age ____ to ____ 4th Opportunities ____

CONTENTS

Preface   7

Part One: The Keys to Finding and Translating Your Personal Numbers

Chapter 1: Discovery   10

Chapter 2: Your Journey Begins   15

Chapter 3: The Soul's Urge   29

Chapter 4: Mind/Personality   43

Chapter 5: The Total Expression   55

Chapter 6: Your Birth Path   71

Chapter 7: Inner Guidance   86

Chapter 8: Your Golden Goal   93

Chapter 9: Karmic Lessons   97

Chapter 10: The Planes of Expression   107

Chapter 11: Challenges and Opportunities   131

Chapter 12: The Master Numbers   150

Chapter 13: The Testing Numbers   159

Chapter 14: Understanding Your Child   164

Chapter 15: Chart Analysis of President George W. Bush   175

Part Two: Your Journey Continues

Chapter 16: Your Address   194

Chapter 17: The Vibratory Significance of 9/11   200

Chapter 18: The Vibratory Secret of Manifestation   205

Bibliography   215

Index   216

About the Author   222

Dedication

*This book is dedicated to
all who seek to know themselves,
and to be an inspiration of good for others.*

Acknowledgments

If it weren't for New Page Books, division of Career Press, this book may never have been written. It is to them I owe heartfelt thanks for giving me the opportunity to write for their new Explorer series. It was their suggestion, and I heartedly agree, that there is a need for a book on numerology that is understandable and fun for the casual reader; one that allows the novice to easily find his/her personal numbers and just as easily interpret them without going into a lot of advanced terminology that leaves them perplexed, and to make for interesting reading as well. I am truly indebted to everyone at Career Press who gave me the opportunity to fill this gap. My special thanks go to the following people:

Ron Fry, Publisher

Michael Lewis, Senior Acquisitions Editor

Stacey Farcas, Editorial Director

Kirsten Beucler, Marketing Associate

Nicole DeFelice, Editor

Each one of them has been right there for me when I needed them. I greatly appreciate each one for without them, this book would not have been written. Thank you. All of you for your part in making this book possible.

Preface

When I was at the start of my journey of discovery, I remember well the questions I had about numerology. Is it a true science, or is it just a toy to dabble with for fun? Does it really tell me truths about myself and answer my own questions about who and what I am, or is it just a game?

I was skeptical at first. But as, I learned, having a first name that starts with an "S" and ending with a "Y," I wouldn't take someone else's opinions. I'd look into it and form my own.

I remember once when Oprah Winfrey had people on the show to debate the authenticity of astrology. The astrologer presented a fine case for it. The other person said that it was stupid for people to waste their time on it. Evidently, he didn't waste his time researching it to see if he might be wrong, because he had no facts to back him up.

The truth is, once anyone really studies it, they can't argue against it. They will find that it is a true science that not only reveals facts about people, but it reveals spiritual laws as well and opens a person's mind to the wonders of our incredible universe and the nature of God.

Just recently, I was a guest on a radio show to discuss my book, *The Secret Science of Numerology.* Off the air, the host told me that a certain fundamentalist preacher wrote a book on all the things he considered as cults, and numerology was one of them. It is obvious that he has preconceived ideas and no knowledge about it. The funny thing is, he is a leader of a "cult" himself. My dictionary defines the word *cult* as "a system of religious rites and observances; zealous devotion to a person or ideal." Then it says, "See religion."

The point of this part of the discussion is this: If we really want to know the authenticity of anything, it is best for us to draw our own conclusions from our own research. That is what I decided to do regarding numerology, and I have never been sorry. What I have learned from this science has benefited me both academically because I learned a great deal about the history of language, alphabets, and philosophers who have shaped our thinking, and of science and the marvelous breakthroughs that have helped us understand the laws of our universe; and spiritually for the greater insight I've gained for knowing these things.

When I attended my first seminar on numerology at the Philosophical Research Society in Los Angeles, I heard several say that numerology would be quicker and easier to learn than astrology, and that is true. But I didn't find it to be as plain as I expected. One thing led to another, and another, and it got deeper and deeper. In searching for the science it was based on, I was drawn into Kabalah, which has a depth that has no end. It is a spiritually revealing, fulfilling, and rewarding study.

And so, to answer my questions at the top: Is numerology a science or a toy to dabble with and have fun? It is a science. And it is also fun to dabble with for there are constant Eurekas and A-has. It stimulates the mind and warms the soul.

Does it tell truths about myself, or is it just a game? By all means, it tells truths. There were things about myself I couldn't understand at all. Numerology revealed my true self to me. I could write a book on those revelations alone, but let's get on with it. Let's talk about you and revealing you to yourself. You are in for a most wonderful adventure.

Part One:

The Keys to Finding and Translating Your
Personal Numbers

Discovery

Many books are written on numerology, so why would you choose this one? There is a need for a beginner's book; one that is very easy to understand, one that will that will help you construct your own chart immediately. In order to keep this as easy as possible, we will first have you find your personal numbers and record them on a chart. Then simply go to the ensuing chapters for each category to find your number and what it has to say about you.

What do we offer that you won't find elsewhere? Briefly, the Inner Guidance Number, the "W" as a part-time vowel that tells you about the "double-you," the "adjective numbers" that precede the root, and, best of all, the science numerology is based upon. In other words, you will learn *why* it works as well as *how* it works.

THE ROOTS OF NUMEROLOGY

This is an ancient science that goes back to antiquity. The principles of numbers and letters have been kept alive in Freemasonry and other secret orders. But it was not adapted for our personal names until the beginning of the 20th century when it was "rediscovered" by a Mrs. L. Dow Balliet of Atlantic City.

Mrs. Balliet was a music teacher who specialized in musical composition. In her study of harmony, she found that the letter name of a musical note and its sound had the same vibration. This correspondence between the letter number and rate of vibration led her to the ancient study of numbers. She proceeded to write several books on the subject, which she called "number vibration," around 1903.

Among her students were Florence Campbell, who later wrote *Your Days are Numbered*, which has remained one of the main handbooks on the subject, and a dentist, Dr. Julia Seton, along with her daughter Juno.

It was Julia Seton who gave the science the new name—numerology—and through her worldwide lectures it became well known. Dr. Seton's dentist daughter, Dr. Juno Jordan, carried on the work by writing several books of her own, lecturing, and founding the California Institute of Numerical Research, where for 25 years numerologists studied and tested their findings. Once their study was complete and they were assured their methods were accurate, the institute was no longer needed and was closed.

THE SCIENCE BEHIND NUMEROLOGY

Yes, there is a real science behind numerology. It is based on physics, the science of the laws governing motion, matter, and energy. In physics, we learn that everything that exists has motion in the realm of vibratory frequency. Everything that exists in the universe from an inert rock and minerals to the organs of your body and the very sound of your name, all have their own distinct rate of vibration. To measure vibration, we need—Tad-dah!—numbers! Numbers are the key to all mysteries because they unlock the vibrational content of any and all things. In a nutshell then, *the secret science behind numerology is that it is based on physics.*

✧ Letters are symbols for sound.

✧ Each sound has a set rate of vibration that can be measured.

✧ Each letter's numbered place in the alphabet *IS* its rate of vibration.

This didn't just happen by chance. The very first alphabet was designed by the greatest scientific and spiritual minds of the day. What Mrs. Dow Balliet discovered in the 20th century, that *the letter name of a musical note and its sound have the same vibration,* is a major secret used by the developers of the alphabet.

Only rabbis had use for the alphabet, for in those ancient times, only the spiritual leaders were educated and taught to read. The spoken language was Aramaic. So the alphabet was used just for their sacred writings. The letters were also their numbers and were placed in order of their rates of vibration, making it a magical alphabet.

In comparing the alphabets, we find that the actual sounds of the Indo-European letters, which stem from Hebrew, are in amazingly the same order as the original alphabets, thus rendering our words as potent as those in the magical alphabets when it comes to numerology. As an example, the third letter in Hebrew is Gimel, G, and our third letter is C, the two pronounced simultaneously (g and c) are produced from the same part of the throat and sound remarkably alike and so forth. If you are really interested in this remarkable science, you will find it spelled out in my book *The Secret Science of Numerology.* But here we want to get to the fun part of self-discovery through charting your name. First, let's take a look at the order of your chart.

THE ORDER OF YOUR CHART

I. Desire/Soul's Urge

Vowels will reveal to you your innermost desires, so it called *Desire*, or your *Soul's Urge*. These inner urgings are the basis of your motivation.

II. Mind/Personality

Consonants clothe the vowels, giving your thoughts and words form. Likewise, they affect the way you act, react, and dress, and they become the you that others see—your personality. It has been called *Mind, Quiescent Self,* and the *Secret Self.* It is your *Personality* that springs forth from your inner thoughts and beliefs.

III. Total Expression

Vowels and consonants combined tell you what your natural abilities and talents are that will lead you to your major accomplishments. This has been called the *Total Expression* and—by some—*Destiny.*

IV. Inner Guidance Number

This number is the frequency we tune to when we go about solving our problems. It is found by doubling your full name number (Total Expression) and adding it down to its root.

V. Birth Path

The number of the month plus the birth day plus the birth year added down to one root number is your *Birth Path*, or *Life Path*.

VI. Golden Goal

There is a number that will give you a clue to what your final fulfillment will be during your senior years. It is found by adding your Total Expression (full name number) to the number of your Birth Path (month, day, and year). This combines the total YOU with your talents and reason for being here. Together they add up to your *Golden Goal*.

VII. Karmic Lessons

Numbers missing in the name.

VIII. Planes of Expression

Physical, Mental, Emotional, Intuitive.

IX. The Challenges and Opportunities

The Challenge shows you the weak links in our life that need to be strengthened. Opportunities are the high spots in your life, the motivating forces that urge you to act on certain impulses in order to achieve your goals. These are found in your Birth Path.

These are the key points we will cover in this book. Inside the cover is a chart you can use for your name numbers. Have paper and pencil handy to figure those numbers as we go along. Graph paper is preferred, but plain paper will do.

Let the journey begin!

Chart 1:
Positive, Negative, and Destructive Aspects of Numbers

	Positive	Negative	Destructive
1 **(Mental)**	Leader. Ambitious. Active. Confident. Inventive. Individual. Thinker. Doer. Works best independently.	Self-conscious. Stubborn. Aggressive. Lazy. Selfish.	Bully. Antagonistic. Bigot. Egotistical. Puts self first at all times.
2 **(Emotional)**	Friendly. Helpful. Tacful and diplomatic. Cooperative. Modest. Neat. Eye for detail.	Insecure. Subservient. Indecisive. Overly emotional. Timid. Easily hurt.	Cruel. Bad temper. Lacks self-control. Sneaky. Deceptive. Liar.
3 **(Emotional)**	Entertainer. Cheerful. Enthusiastic. Humor. Good at writing, speaking, singing.	Vain. Moody. Wasteful. Impulsive. Bored. Dislikes responsibility.	Intolerant. Jealous. Hatred. Gossip. Greed. Pedophile.
4 **(Physical)**	Good worker. Practical. Honest. Organized. Disciplined. Patriotic. Patient. Family lover.	Opinionated. Humorless. Dry. Stern. Narrow-minded. Workaholic. Argumentative.	Hatred. Violent. Vulgar. Jealous. Crude. Animalism.
5 **(Physical)**	Adaptable. Charming. Social. Freedom. Brave. Witty. Adventurous. Supersalesman. Clever.	Irresponsible. Restless. Impatient. Thoughtless.	Perversion. Gambler. Dissipation. Self-indulgence. Debauchery.
6 **(Emotional)**	Humanitarian. Domestic. Nurturer. Responsible. Artistic. Teacher. Musical.	Self-righteous. Smug. Meddlesome. Needs appreciation. Sweet tooth. Mopes. Argues.	Conceit. Domestic or sexual tyranny. Slavery. Drudgery. Nosy and interfering.
7 **(Intuitive)**	Spiritual or scientific. Dignified. Silent. Studious. Intuitive. Educator. Loves nature. Works alone.	Aloof. Unapproachable. Peculiar. Skeptical. Sly. Melancholy. Lives in the past.	Dishonest. Cheat. Gossip. Sarcastic. Faithless. Evil intent. Secret motives.
8 **(Mental)**	Executive ability. Efficient. Ambitious. Good judgement. Ahtletic. Musical. Healthy.	Impatient. Pushy. Thoughtless. Materialistic. Needs philosophic study. Not frugal. Needs to appear prosperous.	Intolerant. Abusive. Schemer. Cruel. Revengeful. Temper. Uncultured. Ingnorant.
9 **(Intuitive)**	Compassionate. Brotherly love. Artistic. Unselfish. Dramatic. Philanthropic.	Overly emotional. Frustrated. Unfulfilled. Burdened. Aimless.	Dissipates. Immoral. Liar. Bad habits. Vulgar. Possessive. Bitter. Morose.
11 **(Mental/** **Intuitive/** **Emotional)**	Inventive. Inspired. Religious leader. Great artist. Idealist. Charming. A special gleam in the eye.	Frustrated. Fanatical. Aimless. Sets goals too high to reach.	Wicked leader. Dishonest. Miserly.
22 **(Very** **Emotional)**	Master achiever. Good at details. Powerful.	Narrow. Uncultured. Inferiority complex. Disapproval.	Wicked. Ulterior motives. Reckless. Black magic. Gang leader.
33 **(Very** **Emotional)**	Compassion. Deep understanding. Empathetic. Gentle. Kind. Loving service. Nurturer. Selfless giving. Unpretentious.	Burdened. Careless. Overpowering sweet tooth.	Martyr. Meddlesome. Slave to others. Slovenly.

Your Journey Begins

You are about to embark on the most exciting journey of your life—the one to your inner self—to learn why you are as you are. Don't you ever ask yourself, *Why am I like this? Why do I react this way?* If you are like most of us, there are certain things you just don't understand about yourself. If you follow the easy directions in this book, you will learn more about yourself than you could believe possible. And you won't want to stop there. You'll want to understand your family members and friends, too. You are holding in your hands the keys to reveal your character, tendencies, desires, and much more.

Use your Birth Name as it is on your birth certificate, but eliminate any after titles or numbers such as Jr. and III. That is the vibration you came in on and holds all the information on your character, desires, and your physical, mental, emotional, and intuitive planes of being. That name in numerology is as important as your birth date and time of birth in astrology. It is your personal code. The names you use later definitely have influence. It's like changing your hair color: The effect will be different, but underneath it all, the roots come out in their natural color.

If your name includes a "W" you just may have a special calling. It really is "the double-you," for at some point in your life, another desire springs forth and may take you in a different direction.

The letters W and Y are considered as consonants by most numerologists. The rule is that all vowels have phonic value, whereas consonants do not.

The W is always a vowel when it gives the delicate "oo" sound. In every case where this subtle vowel sound occurs, I have found that more significant information can be gleaned when W is used first as a consonant and then as a vowel, giving a double Soul's Urge. This means that if you have a W in the name where it has that delicate "oo" sound, as in William, you will have two separate Soul's Urges, two distinct Desires. It is not a vowel when it has no phonic value, which is before R, as in wrist, or when used internally, as in answer and two. When the W rises to a vowel, the consonants are changed too, changing the Mind/Personality number. (See Chart 2.)

There may be words where the Y has no phonic value, but I have not found a name where it does not add the "ee" sound, even when preceded by an "E," so I always use it as a vowel in names.

Let's start now. On a regular 8 x 11 paper held horizontally, write your complete Birth Name down a few spaces from the upper left. First we will find all your main numbers, taking one faction at a time to make it less complicated. Then place each number on the chart provided for you at the beginning of the book.

I. VOWELS: SOUL'S URGE OR DESIRE

The vowels and their numbers are: **A E I O U Y**

The sometimes vowel is:
$$1\ 5\ 9\ 6\ 3\ 7$$
W
5

You will place these numbers above the vowels of your name. We'll use an imaginary name as an example.

  6   5   1 3   6   5 = 26/8   Soul's Urge = 8
R O B E R T P A U L J O N E S

Add each of those numbers. They come to 26. The root of 26 is **8** (2+6=8).

So 8 is the vibratory rate of his Soul's Urge, or Desire. Do the same with *your* name and enter your root number for your vowels after Soul's Urge, or Desire if you prefer. If you have a W, you will count it as a consonant first and use that number as the first Soul's Urge, in this manner:

1	7	9		=17/8	1st Soul's Urge = 8
1		7 5 9		= 22	2nd Soul's Urge = 22

M A R Y   W I C K

Note 1: You will have two columns instead of one because of the W (see the W chart).

Note 2: Also note that we did not reduce the 22 to a 4. This is because all numbers that are doubled, such as 11, 22, 33, 44, 55, 66, 77, 88, and 99 are considered as *Master* Numbers and are not reduced. All Master Numbers are powerful because they accentuate themselves and their root number, as in 11/2, 22/4, 33/6, and so forth. *Read more about the master numbers in Chapter 12.* Now we will find your Personality number from the consonants.

II. CONSONANTS: MIND OR SECRET SELF THAT MAKES UP YOUR PERSONALITY

This number will tell you about the way you think and dress.

Using this chart, write the number of the consonant letters *underneath* your Birth Name, as in the example:

1	2	3	4	5	6	7	8	9
A	B	C	D	E	F	G	H	I
J	K	L	M	N	O	P	Q	R
S	T	U	V	W	X	Y	Z	

R O B E R T   P A U L   J O N E S
9 2 9 2 7   3 1   5   1 = 39 3 + 9= 12/3

Add each of these numbers together and they come to 39. Then add again. 3+9= 12/**3**.

If you have that W, it will change here, too:

M A R Y   W I C K
4   9   5   3   2 = 23 2+3= 5   1st Personality – 5
4   9   3   2 = 18 1 + 8= 9 2nd Personality – 9

III. VOWELS AND CONSONANTS COMBINED: TOTAL EXPRESSION OR DESTINY

This number will tell you your natural abilities and talents.

For **Robert Paul Jones** then, we add the total of the vowels, **8**, to the total of the consonants, **11**, giving us **10/1**, and write it on the chart under the last entry as:

Expression = **1**

For **Mary Wick** there will now be a single number. Whether you add The 1st Soul's Urge and 1st Personality together: 8+5 = 13/4, or the 2nd Soul's Urge and the 2nd Personality together: 22 plus 9 = 31/4, the Total Expression remains **4**.

So far, the charts will look like this:

Robert Paul Jones   Soul's Urge – 26/**8**
                        Personality – 39/12/3
                        Expression – **11**

Mary Wick   1st Soul's Urge – 17/**8**   2nd Soul's Urge – **22**
                Personality – 23/**5**   Personality – 18/**9**
                Expression – 13/**4**   Expression – 31/**4**

As you can see, both Robert and Mary have the Soul's Urge of 8. There is a difference though, and that is in the numbers added to get to that 8; the Adjective Numbers.

Robert – **26/8**
Mary –**17/8** (which raises to Master Number **22**)

The Adjective Numbers

Those numbers behind the 8 are the adjectives that further define the Soul's Urge. An 8 wants success and has the ambition to accomplish great things. They have great stamina and good health, so this is part of the desire. Robert's 2 and 6 reveal that he desires his success to come by working with or for others, paying attention to detail (2), and artistic qualities (6), and through the voice in his career (6). Mary's 1 and 7 want her to succeed on her own. She prefers to work alone and use her own ideas. The 1 is independent, confident, and a doer, whereas the 7 thinks things through and works best alone. They show that she prefers to excel in a chosen profession and will study hard to achieve her goals. If the background numbers were 44, it would mean doubly practical, honest, and working overtime to achieve.

At this point, you may want to stop and see what your first three name numbers have to say about you in Chapters 3, 4, and 5.

IV. THE INNER GUIDANCE NUMBER

The Inner Guidance Number is the frequency we tune to when we go about solving our problems.

Now that you have your Total Expression number, it is very simple to find your Inner Guidance Number. Either add the three columns or simply double the Total Expression.

Robert Paul Jones

Soul's Urge	**8**	
Personality	**+ 3**	
Total Expression = $\underline{11 + 11} = 22$		**Inner Guidance = 22**
22		

For Robert, adding the column gives us **22**. Doubling his Total Expression also gives us **22**. For Mary, the root is 8 either way.

1st Soul's Urge	**8**	2nd Soul's Urge	**22**
Personality	**+ 5**	Personality	**+ 5**
Total Expression =	$\underline{4}$	**Total Expression** =	$\underline{4}$
	17/8		**35/8**

Inner Guidance = 8

When you know your Inner Guidance Number, go to Chapter 7 and read the two definitions for your number. The first is the way you naturally solve your problems when your brain emits beta waves, as it does in waking moments, and the second gives you a practical meditation to use in solving them. In meditation the brain emits alpha waves, which open your consciousness to receive your inner counsel.

Before we go on to the other name numbers, let's take the next major point on your chart: your Birth Path.

V. THE BIRTH PATH

The Birth Path shows what you are here to do.

The number of your birth month, plus the birth day, plus the birth year added down to one root number is your *Birth Path*, or *Life Path*. The months are numbered in their order, starting with January.

1. January	5. May	9. September
2. February	6. June	10. October
3. March	7. July	11. November
4. April	8. August	12. December

This can be added one of two ways. For example, July 27, 1966. Convert the month to 7. Then add across: $7 + 2 + 7 + 1 + 9 + 6 + 6 = 38/11$. Birth Path is 11. Or consider the 19 in 1966 as a 1 because $1+9$ is 10, and $1+0 = 1$. Then we would add more simply, $7+2+7+1+6+6 = 29/11$. Either way will get you to the Birth Path number. Write this number underneath the Total Expression.

Let's say this is Robert's Birthday: $7/27/1966 = 29/$ **11,** and Mary's is $11/26/1967$, which added across is $24/6.$

Robert Paul Jones

Soul's Urge	8
Personality	3
Total Expression	11
Birth Path	**11**

Inner Guidance = 22

Mary Wick

1st Soul's Urge	8	2nd Soul's Urge	22	
Personality	5	Personality	9	Inner Guidance = 8
Total Expression	4	Total Expression	4	
Birth Path	**6**			

This is the way their charts will look so far. Place yours in the same area on your chart, and check Chapter 6 for the description of your Birth Path.

For the sake of the chart, the easiest one to take next is the Golden Goal.

VI. Golden Goal

This tells what your final fulfillment will be in your golden years after retirement.

There is a number that will give you a clue to what your final fulfillment will be. It is found by adding your Total Expression (full name number) to the number of your Birth Path (month, day, and year). This combines the total YOU with your talents and reason for being here. Together they add up to your *Golden Goal* (some call it Reality). Place this number to the right of the Birth Path underneath the Inner Guidance. For Robert and Mary it will look like this:

Robert Paul Jones

Total Expression	11
Birth Path	11
	22 Golden Goal

Mary Wick

Total Expression	4
Birth Path	6
	10 (1) Golden Goal

The Golden Goals are given in Chapter 8.

The Inclusion Table

From here on we will use only Robert as an example. Underneath the last entries, Birth Path and Golden Goal, at the left side write "Inclusion Table." Have your name before you with the vowels' numbers above and the consonants' numbers below. Count all the 1s and place that number under the 1. Do the same with each number, as shown:

(Note: Count the numbers you inserted, and then letters in your name. They must agree. There are 15 letters in Robert's name.)

```
      6  5     1 3    6  5
     R O B E R T  P A U L  J O N E S
      9  2   9 2 7    3 1   5   1
```

Inclusion Table
1	2	3	4	5	6	7	8	9
3	2	2	–	3	2	1	–	2

4 and 8 = Karmic Lessons

VII. KARMIC LESSON(S)

Our weak areas that need to be strengthened.

Directly under the Inclusion Table, write the missing number(s). Here, they are 4 and 8. Those are the Karmic Lessons, the vibrations missing from the name. (*See Chapter 9.*)

VIII. THE PLANES OF EXPRESSION

Each number and its corresponding letters represent a vibration that is related to one of four planes:

Physical 4, 5
4 (DMV) and 5 (ENW)

Emotional 2, 3, 6
2 (BKT) and 3 (CLU) and 6 (FOX)

Metal 1, 8
1 (AJS) and 8 (HQZ)

Intuitive 7, 9
7 (GPY) and 9 (IR)

First we need a brief explanation of these planes. The way we balance these four aspects of our nature is a clue to our own true character and vocational aptitudes. It is the many combinations of these qualities that make each of us unique. Briefly they are:

Physical

The 4s (D, M, V) and the 5s (E, N, W). This shows our physical endurance, dexterity, and energies. It is concerned with material matters and natural instincts.

Mental

The 1s (A, J, S) and the 8s (H, Q, Z). This shows the way we reason and whether we are analytical, creative, or curious.

Emotional

The 2s (B, K, T), the 3s (C, L, U), and the 6s (F, O, X). This shows how we deal with our feelings and how we express them. It reveals how we handle our attitudes.

Intuitive

The 7s (letters G, P, Y) and the 9s (letters I, R). This shows the higher nature that senses the abstract impressions, imagination, spiritual outlook, and the awareness of an inner guidance.

When you determine your numbers and have placed them in your chart, read about your characteristics in the charts on the planes, starting on page 110.

Now add this to your chart.

1. Add the letters to the Inclusion Table. Three or more of the same letter shows that those traits are strong.

2. To the right of the Inclusion Table, write "The Planes of Expression." Under that, list the planes. Then we will determine what number we place after each plane. We will use Robert as an example. As we do so, figure your name and place your numbers and letters on your chart as follows:

Inclusion Table								
1	2	3	4	5	6	7	8	9
3	2	2	-	3	2	1	-	2
A	B	U		E	O	P		R
J	T	L		E	O			R
S		N						

The Planes of Expression

Physical - **3**
Mental - **3**
Emotional - **6**
Intuitive - **3**
4 and 8 = Karmic Lessons

Physical

Count the numbers under the 4 and the 5. For Robert there are no 4s and three 5s. So, after Physical, we write 3.

Mental

Count the numbers under the 1 and the 8. Robert has three 1s and no 8s. So, after Mental, we write 3.

Emotional

Count the numbers under the 2, 3, and 6. Robert has two 2s, two 3s, and two 6s. So, we write 6 after Emotional.

Intuitive

Count the numbers under the 7 and the 9. Robert has one 7 and two 9s. We place that 3 after Intuitive.

IX. THE CHALLENGES AND OPPORTUNITIES

The Challenge shows us the difficulties we must learn to deal with. Opportunities are motivating forces that urge us to act on certain impulses in order to achieve our goals. These are found in our birth date. We will use Robert's birth date, July 27, 1966 as an example.

Challenges

First, reduce the month, day, and year to its root. The month of July–7. The day is 27: 2 +7 =9. So the root of the day is 9. The year is 1966: add 1 + 9 + 6 + 6 = 22. Then add the 2+ 2=4, which determines the year. The root of the day or year is one case where the Master Number's root is used. It will look like this: 7-9-4.

To find each challenge, subtract the month from the day and the day from the year, always the small numbers from the larger.

To clarify:

First challenge: 9 - 7 = **2** (day minus month, *smaller from larger number*).

Second Challenge: 9 - 4 = **5** (day minus year).

Third Challenge: 5 - 2 = **3** (subtract first two challenges).

Fourth and main Challenge: 7 - 4 = **3** (month minus year).

Place them in this fashion:

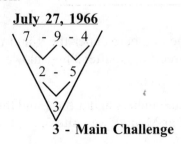

July 27, 1966

3 - Main Challenge

Opportunities

These are also called Pinnacles and are found by adding the birth dates in the same way as we subtracted them for the Challenges. Only this time, the numbers will be placed above the birth date. (Always add two numbers down to the root as shown.)

To clarify:

1st Opportunity: 7+9= 16. Then 1+6 = **7** (month plus day).

2nd Opportunity: 9+4= 13. Then 1+3= **4** (day plus year).

3rd Opportunity: 7+4= **11** (total of 1st and 2nd Opportunities).

4th and main Opportunity: 7+4= **11** (month plus year).

Place them in this fashion, above the Challenges:

11 Main Opportunity

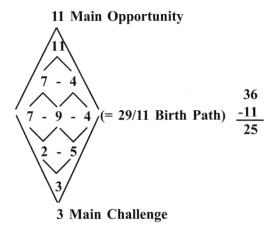

3 Main Challenge

To more easily read them, we move those numbers to a table with the challenges on the left, Opportunities on the right, and your age placed in the center. To find your age at the end of the first cycle, subtract your Birth Path from 36. There are four main cycles throughout our lives where we have peaks of attainment, or opportunities, and our weaknesses or challenges coincide with these. Nine is the end of a complete cycle, so the number 36, which is 4x9, is important in calculating them. To find the peak of the first cycle in our own life, we subtract our own Birth Path number from 36, as shown above. Once you determine that number, place it in the top line as "Birth to age ___." (In this case, subtract the 11 from 25, the length of the 1st cycle.)

Challenges	Age	Opportunities
2	Birth to age 25	7
5	25 - 34	4
3	34 - 43	11
Main Challenge 3	43 - on	11 Main Opportunity

See page 132 for the interpretation of the Challenges, and page 140 for the Opportunities.

NUMBER INTENSITIES

Look over all the numbers in your chart. If you have more than three of any one number, that vibration is strong in your life. If there is a number that is missing completely, that is one that may be holding you back. There are two ways to deal with that. First, add the number to your name. If it is a 4, you need to add a D, M, or V.

Or, read about that number and work to establish its positive traits in your daily life. For example, if you are missing a 4, in number or letter, you need to learn how to get organized, care more for your family, discipline yourself, and be more honest.

Now that you have all your numbers on your chart, you can interpret them by the meanings of the numbers. The next eight chapters will aid you in each category.

You can stop at the end of this first section and have a pretty good idea of what your name and birth date have to say about you. But if your interest is piqued and you want to know more about the hidden meanings of numbers and letters, you will find interesting information with all of the Cabalistic detail and Biblical references in my book *The Secret Science of Numerology*.

Chart 2:
Sample Numerology Chart
Robert Paul Jones
7/27/1966 = 29/11

  6 5   1 3   6   5   = 26/8 = Soul's Urge **8**

R O B E R T P A U L J O N E S

9   2   9 2 7   3 1   5   1 = 39/12/3 = Personality **3**

= Expression **11**

= Inner Guidance **22**

= Birth Path **11**

= Golden Goal **22**

Inclusion Table

1	2	3	4	5	6	7	8	9
3	2	2	--	3	2	1	--	2
A	B	U		E	O	P		R
J	T	L		E	O			R
S		N						

4 and 8 = Karmic Lessons

The Planes of Expression
Physical - **3** EEN
Mental - **3** AJS
Emotional - **6** BTULOO
Intuitive - **3** RRP

	Challenges	Age	Opportunities	
	2	Birth to age 25	7	
	5	25 - 34	4	
	3	34 - 43	11	
Main Challenge	3	43 - on	11	Main Opportunity

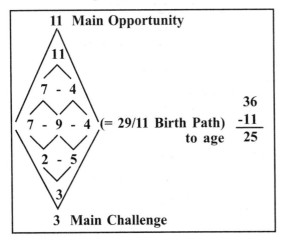

11 Main Opportunity

11

7 - 4

7 - 9 - 4 (= 29/11 Birth Path)

2 - 5

3

36
−11
25

to age

3 Main Challenge

Chart 3:
The Double-You

As the 23rd letter, the W has a deep emotional nature, for numbers 2 and 3 are emotional numbers. Their root total, 5, represents the five physical senses. Overindulging in sensual pleasures or expressing any of the negative traits of the 5. is living in the pits of the W. (Notice the W's three peaks and two pits). The W is also known as *the spiritual letter* because of the great victory achieved when one raises oneself from the depths of despair. When the person learns that the true meaning of the 5's freedom is to be responsible for their own actions, the W is raised in vibration and takes on the qualities of responsibility and gentleness.

Adding the W (5) to the Vowels	
Soul's Urge/Desire	
1 becomes 6	Thinks less of self and is more caring for others; may consider having a family.
2 becomes 7	No longer a follower, now desires to specialize in a career, to achieve perfection through study, or to grow spiritually.
3 becomes 8	Has more power, is better organized, and no longer scatters energies.
4 becomes 9	Once its own foundation is secure, seeks to help others and be more aware of others' needs and feelings.
5 becomes 10	The senses are under control. It now has a spiritual mission to fulfill.
6 becomes 11	Becomes more intuitive, artistic, and/or spiritual. Tends to daydream.
7 becomes 3	From introvert to extrovert, the inner knowledge bursts forth into beautiful self expression.
8 becomes 4	From striving to manifestation.
9 becomes 5	From tests well done to seeking knowledge on yet a higher plane.

Subtracting the W (5) From the Consonants	
Personality/The way you appear to others	
1 becomes 5	From unique and distinguished to versatile and daring.
2 becomes 6	From very neat and fussy or plain to casual and comfortable.
3 becomes 7	From colorful and lots of jewelry to well-dressed and conservative.
4 becomes 8	From suits and practical clothes to the business-success look.
5 becomes 9	From versative and daring to comfortable and casual.
6 becomes 10	From casual to dignified and individual.
7 becomes 11	Stays well-dressed and conservative, but also upscale casual.
8 becomes 3	From business-success look to freer-flowing styles and more color.
9 becomes 4	From comfortable and casual to suits and practical clothes.

The Soul's Urge

YOUR VOWELS

The world's oldest religions teach that people can unite with God through the chant, through the singing of hymns, or by intoning the meditational "OM." Somehow they knew that vowels set up a vibration that connects our inner response with that of our Creator. Each sound has an individual vibratory pattern that can be measured.

The rate of vibration changes with each vowel sound, giving each one a different numerical value. The grouping of vowels gives each name its individuality, its own tone, and the characteristics that are included with that vibratory tone. Within that vibration is found the inner desires of the soul, the ever-lasting self. This deeper desire clarifies your motives for what you really want out of life. It even tells you what your positive attitudes are that help you carry out this wish and the negative attitudes that block your progress.

There are no bad numbers. But just as there is a backside for every front, there are positive and negative aspects to every number vibration. Through the power of choice, we sample a little of each as we journey through life. Our numbers reveal to us our tendencies, and it is up to us to choose how we react to every situation. If we choose the positive side most of the time, we will meet with success. When we opt for the negative, we are shutting off the flow of the universal creative energy and thereby cause our own limitations, drawbacks, and negative experiences that ultimately complicate our lives.

Therefore, our life experiences are *not* pre-ordained. All of our accomplishments, successes, and failures are of our own making. Knowing our numbers makes it easier to understand ourselves so it will be easier to make the right decisions to fulfill the urgings of our soul's desires.

1 SOUL'S URGE OR DESIRE

Ones have a desire to excel, for they are born leaders and can never be happy in a subordinate position. They are doers, not watchers, and they love to win whether it is in sports, business, or love.

Pride, sensitivity, charm and wit are all a part of 1's make-up. Ideas are creative and original. People look to them to lead the way, for they have an aura of inner power and determination. They desire to lead, and as leaders they don't want to infringe on anyone's rights for they believe in fair play. If you have a 1 Soul's Urge and are the unselfish type who considers the feelings of others, people will love and respect you and want to help you all they can. For you, life is full of opportunities.

The inner desire to stand out in your line of work or hobby will happen when you work towards your goal with your natural assets of self-confidence and initiative. The 1 makes you so idealistic that you can be easily hurt. Otherwise, you are positive and determined. Clear thinking is inherent in you. By expressing these qualities in a positive way, you can become a respected and loved boss or leader.

The negative side of the 1 is falling into the trap of self-importance and not being considerate of the feelings of others. The extreme is being tyrannical, bossy, arrogant, and conceited, and by holding much resentment: all traits that cause tension and unhappiness.

With a 1 Soul's Urge, you definitely sense your own uniqueness and are aware that the majority of people are not as strong in their accomplishments as you are. You notice that so many people are ordinary, and some so disturbingly dull—to your way of thinking—that it is easy to become overly bossy. You really have to be careful not to look down on those people, for that attitude will be reflected on your face and in your mannerisms, resulting in unattractive qualities.

To overcome this type of negativity, it will help to realize what a force for good you can be in those people's lives. You can set an example by your own good words and actions.

2 Soul's Urge or Desire

This is probably the kindest vibration of all, for 2s have a loving, giving nature with the desire to bring peace and harmony to every situation. Their desire for harmony reflects in everything they do. They love to help those in need and to inspire, love, guide, and protect people. They clearly see both points of view, and this gives them the ability to resolve things in a calm and tactful manner. They can calm ruffled feathers for they understand people's feelings. These gentle, loving ways make them good companions and exceptionally fine diplomats.

If you have the 2 Soul's Urge, you are highly sensitive, care deeply, and would never knowingly hurt anyone. Because of this, you may appear shy or self-conscious. Those who know you love you, and you have many friends. You must be careful not to let others take advantage of your good nature, though.

It is not your nature to get involved in brawls. Dignity is part of the personality of the 2 vibration. You prefer seeing people at their best and you hate vulgarity and crudeness. Those base, low vibrations hit a sensitive nerve, making you very uncomfortable. The beauty of art, music, and love has the power to restore the harmonious balance that is vital to your well-being. Overall, the 2 Desire in you needs and wants love.

That 2 Desire gives you the need to have someone appreciate what you are able to do. When it comes to work, you are far happier working quietly in the background, attending to details, for you have the ability to perfect every feature of your work and it is easier for you to do your best when undisturbed. You are able to handle small objects with ease and are happiest in an occupation where you can use this ability.

You love music and the arts and will have the urge to study the intricacies of either one or both. You would make a fine specialized musician because of your great sensitivities and attention to detail. It is the same with art. Your deep feelings and keen sense of detail, when directed into artistic endeavors, will give you a feeling of great satisfaction and fulfillment. Your home has a place for everything and everything in its place, unless you are at the negative side of the spectrum.

The negative 2 is the opposite. You are messy, do not trust your own decisions, are overly emotional, and are too nit-picky over details. The urge to collect things can result in "collecto-mania" (kleptomania). Very negative 2s are sneaky and quite proficient as liars.

11/2

Eleven is known as "The Psychic Master." Even as a child they seemed to have their own standard of ideals and thoughts about God, life, and what is right and wrong. The positive 11 feels a great inner strength and desires to use it to bring light to the world, to lift and improve mankind. Are you an 11? Then your concern is to better the world as a whole rather than one person at a time. Some accomplish this as powerful ministers or teachers, others through their artwork, and some through their acting/musical/creative abilities. There is a chance for fame in your chosen field.

The negative 11 finds a thrill in exerting personal power over others. An 11 is either good or evil, and the evil type can be quite cruel. You are overly sensitive, tense, impatient, and snobbish.

3 SOUL'S URGE OR DESIRE

Three's deepest desire is to express creative talents in a way that will lift, enrich, and entertain others. Their zest for life is catchy, for they exude a bright and cheerful disposition. They really like to make people happy. People will gather around to listen to them, for they express themselves in an entertaining manner. They enjoy being noticed, and they really want to be the best in their profession. They have so much artistic creativity that they can only be happy when allowed to pursue these abilities. But they need a 4 or 8 for a manager!

If you have the 3 Desire, you entertain with style. Everyone has a good time. You have such a flair for life that people either love you or are jealous of you. And you are always in love. Children are attracted to you for they sense the love you feel for them and appreciate and need your light-hearted attitude.

The artistic nature of your 3 Desire seeks beautiful surroundings. Dull and drab places affect you adversely, but nevermind; your creative imagination is sheer inspiration. You can take drab surroundings and put beauty into them, find a sad face and make it smile. You have a song in your heart and inspiration in your soul. You have a way with words that makes it easy for you to communicate your thoughts. Writing comes easy for you.

Physical labor is not one of your desires. You want your job to be artistic or fun, more like play than work. People get the feeling that you don't take life seriously, and sometimes you don't. You aren't always bubbly and talkative. There is a quiet side too. This happens when you draw into yourself to recharge your batteries of effervescence.

The negative side of the 3 is too sensitive to criticism. You tend to talk too much, say things you shouldn't say, gossip, and even bore people. You desire marriage, but often are often attracted to the wrong types. You don't always know what you are looking for in a mate, and that leads to separations and divorce. There is no innate happiness in the truly negative 3, but you desire it with all your heart.

Note: Occasionally I will comment on the background numbers of the root, to give the idea of their meanings as adjectives for the root.

12/3

The independence and leadership ability of the 1 takes precedence. Yet, the 2 loves companionship, is sensitive, and prefers soft, romantic music, and peaceful situations. You are considerate, have a tactful approach, and appreciate the same in others.

21/3

Companionship and sensitivity from the 2 with your preference of soft, romantic music and peaceful situations comes first. You are considerate and have a tactful approach, and you appreciate the same in others. The 1 shows your innate strength and independent character. You have your own unique ambitions and find great pleasure in doing things in your own way. Together, the energies of 1 and 2 supply the joy that is found in 3.

48/12/3

The 4 gives you a great sense of patriotism, love of family, and traditional values. It is your utmost desire to feel that you are stable in your life. Security is important to you, and that means emotional as well as financial. The 8 adds good judgment and a need to have your physical life in perfect balance with the spiritual, so knowledge of philosophy is important. You will argue a fact and must learn to control your temper.

4 SOUL'S URGE OR DESIRE

One of the 4's profound desires is for financial security. They are happiest when they can plan ahead and do everything exactly right, right down to the detail. To take an idea and put it to practical use is the 4's idea of accomplishment, and 4s do have managerial abilities. Many with a 4 Soul's Urge have a desire to teach.

If this is your Soul's Urge number, you are honest, practical, serious, hardworking, determined, and reliable. You will apply yourself and enjoy doing so because you have great confidence in yourself, are disciplined, and love to see the results of your efforts. Being well organized and practical does have its merits; it helps you attain the secure foundation you desire. When you are sure of yourself, you believe in your own opinions to the point of argument. But it is also your desire to deal fairly with others.

When it comes to your work, you know what to do and how to do it and resent any authority telling you how it should be done. Just leave you in peace to do your work at your own pace and you are happy.

The 4 is a family-oriented vibration: loyal, loving, and devoted, but doesn't always show it. You will find you are happiest when you decide not to make a big deal of the little things, because it is a tendency to fret and worry about everything being perfect, right down to petty details. It is wonderful to be able to have everything just right when you have no one to please but yourself, but it can be difficult in a relationship.

Negative 4s can be narrow-minded, cocky, headstrong, bossy, and stubborn. They can become so entrenched in their projects that they lose sight of the fact that they need time out for fun and relaxation. In other words, 4 is a workaholic!

22

This is a Master Number known as "The Master Architect." This vibration is one that wants to do things on a big scale, or accomplish a major goal. It is probably the strongest of all desires because of its increased power. You see and feel things more acutely because of the sensitivity of the double 2, so details stand out to you where others don't even notice them. You may desire to handle small objects and create things of beauty with your hands or build something on a large scale for everyone to use and enjoy.

5 SOUL'S URGE OR DESIRE

Freedom is greatly valued. Fives want to enjoy life fully and be free to come and go as they wish and do anything when they feel like it. If 5 is your Soul's Urge, love and companionship are important to you, and you do make a wonderful partner for someone as long as you have your freedom intact. If anyone holds on to you too tightly, your urge will be to run away. But the person who respects your freedom and trusts you will have you as a faithful partner for life.

You want to know everything because part of the 5 vibration is the desire for knowledge. It equips you with a good mind, a keen imagination, and a wonderful sense of creativity, and you enjoy using the facts you discover. You have a strong desire to travel, meet new people, and learn new things. But when you travel, you don't want to go where the tourists go. You like to wander where the natives are and learn to speak with them in their own language.

You like to get where you are going quickly. Sometimes you drive too fast. Some of you take to racing cars or boats—anything where speed is involved.

Variety is the spice of your life. Get out often, enjoy the sunshine, and be with lots of people to exchange ideas and try new things. All this is important to fulfill the Soul's Urge of the 5.

With all this desire for new experiences, rest assured that you are adaptable and versatile. Your enthusiasm fills a room. Those who have the 5 Desire make fine salespeople because their sheer enthusiasm over a product and can sell it to someone who doesn't even need it.

Negative 5's attitudes are a lack of patience and having a difficult time accepting responsibilities. Domestic duties are fine as long as they don't feel expected to do them. Restlessness overtakes them when they feel trapped in a situation or having to do a routine job. Their mind will jump from one interest to another, and they want the freedom to drop what they are doing and move on to the next activity when they feel like it.

Whenever you feel trapped or in a rut, it will be helpful to buy a new outfit, go to an amusement park, take a short trip, or take an early vacation. A change of pace is always healing for you.

23/5

If these are the background numbers for the root of your 5 vowels, the 2 shows your sensitivity and emotional side. You are deeply touched by kindness and cry easily at hurts. The 3 shows the need for verbal communication and ways to express your creativity.

6 SOUL'S URGE OR DESIRE

Sixes are romantic. They desire to bring love and happiness to everyone. The desire for home, family, and roots is strong. They want responsibility, are faithful, true, and honest, and expect the same of their mate. There is a nurturing instinct that makes them a sort of *cosmic parent*. They are the type to adopt children, take in stray animals, or give loving care to the aged. Or they may be the one who desires to teach important fundamentals to the young.

The 6 represents the voice in the career, and when this is your desire you may not mind taking part in community projects to have a say in what is done to make things better. You want to see the law upheld and justice done, because you have very strong feelings for what is right or wrong. Many who have the 6 Desire would be fine politicians or public servants because the inner response is to public needs with a desire to make everything right.

This quality also makes you an excellent advice-giver. There is something about you that makes people feel they can confide in you, sensing that you will know the answers to their problems. And you do. Your open-minded and understanding manner makes you very comfortable to talk to. Once you are home, you want to be relaxed and at ease. You dress casually and have a favorite chair. You like your choice of artwork in your home to enjoy and inspire you.

The influence of the 6 is what makes you desire to use your artistic and healing abilities. Here we find fine singers, artists, publishers, nurses, and doctors. You have a good sense of color, and as an artist, you create the loveliest handwork. As caregivers, you provide the most loving and compassionate care. With a vowel count of 6, you are a soft touch, sensitive to people's needs, and you want to heal every wound. Your desire is to heal, to teach, and to serve.

Is there a negative side? You bet. The 6 cares so much about family and friends that it is possible to overdo in their affections and smother them. The 6 has high ideals and likes to see everyone live up to them, so the hardest thing for a 6 is to let other people have their own way, for a 6 is so sure it is right that it becomes too smug. That smugness can out-picture negatively into a demanding and bossy nature and will use force to have its way. Then we have domestic tyranny. All 6s must learn to not be quite so personal, and to respect other people's ways, ideas, and desires. Negative 6s can't take criticism. It causes them distress and agitation. They need praise for what they do. They need peace and harmony to the point that they cannot take harsh noises or rude interruptions. Those things will set them off.

33/6

This is a Master Number, a high vibration of spiritual love, because with it comes the deep feelings of compassion. People sense this quality in you and are drawn to you. In return, you do your best to uplift them. At times you feel as though you really are here to do something special for the world. You have a wonderful imagination that stimulates your creative abilities. As a result, you are deeply moved by things of beauty, whether it is someone's artwork or the natural wonders of nature. You love and need time alone away from the city and crowds, to bask in the beauty and quiet of the country. It is not always easy to live in this high vibration. You'll have such a strong need to be appreciated, and often there will be responsibilities that cause anxiety. With fear comes inner turmoil and the inability to make decisions.

7 SOUL'S URGE OR DESIRE

The 7 is known as *The Thinker* because of its analytical mind. Unlike any other number, the 7 will evaluate and think out anything of importance and form its own conclusions rather than blindly accept anyone else's ideas. Its desire is to always seek out the hidden facts. Sevens are skeptical and will ask questions. They are very conservative. They would rather remain silent than say anything to hurt anyone's feelings.

If you have the 7 Desire, you don't want anyone bothering you with frivolous things, as you hate to waste your time on things of little importance. But if they give you the facts to back up their statements, you will listen intently. Then you need time alone to process that information.

You love to read and have a great need for higher education, for you desire to be dedicated to a profession. You are happiest if you can be considered the expert. Here we find dedicated scientists, religious and political leaders, architects, lawyers, professors, expert cooks and bakers, and artists of all types who desire to bring their own creative beauty into the world. Whereas a 6 Desire will be part of the general practitioner's makeup, the one with the 7 Desire will prefer to specialize.

You desire love and understanding. In relationships, you can be one of the most charming people. You do need rest and time alone so, if you marry, your spouse must be aware of those needs. You have a special dignity about you that makes you stand out in a crowd. You are comfortable among people you know and respect. With them you can be full of fun and very witty, but you can be very aloof and distant with strangers or those whom you feel have nothing to offer other than small talk.

Crowds don't appeal to you. It is doubtful you'd like to be at a ball game—unless you are the player. The opera is a different story. There one attends something that offers dedicated artists who have studied hard to achieve a magnificent voice, and the crowds who attend are usually like-minded people who appreciate artistry.

Negative 7s just hate to be asked questions. They can be very cold and aloof, even unapproachable. They are so sensitive, they will brood a great deal if they have not lived up to their own expectations, especially if they lack the education to have helped them succeed in a profession. They will nurse their grievances. Many turn to drink or drugs out of their frustrations and fears. They are secretive and do not want to reveal their innermost thoughts to anyone.

43/7

The 4 emphasizes the basic honesty present in this 7. Jokes don't go over too well, but a true story with a funny ending will delight this person to no end. The 4 appreciates family and is dedicated to supporting it. The 3 loves children and wants to give them the best of everything. Three loves being happy and making others happy. Inside a 7, the 3 may not burst out with a loud laugh, but the twinkle in the eye is there.

8 Soul's Urge or Desire

The desire of 8s is to be very successful and have all the material goodies to show for it. If they haven't achieved monetary success, they want to at least look as though they have, and they are always well groomed. Positive 8s radiate power and vitality. They want to attain money through their own initiative even if it means to marry into wealth. And even then, they want the mate to be of strong character and to possess the same ambitions. The 8 can be warm and loving, but the desire for success doesn't give them much time for romance.

The 8 is a mental number vibration. It wants to achieve its wealth through planning, organizing, and directing, but not do the physical labor. If you have the 8 Desire, you just hate to take orders from anyone else, so you should be the corporate leader or the head of your own business. You enjoy making plans and having others follow through with them. You work hard for what you desire and want money for the protection it will afford you in your senior years.

You don't mind the opposition, for you are confident and determined. Because of your enthusiasm, poise, and excellent judgment, you can be a tremendous power for good. On the road to successful attainment there will be some rough times because you are so hard on yourself. But courage and vitality will see you through. The rewards are greater for you when you work for beneficial goals rather than personal power.

Many with the 8 Desire vibration are drawn to sports, for the 8 is physically fit and strong and is found on the winning team. Many 8s don't care for sports at all, but are interested in music as a career, to play an instrument or sing. Whichever you are, you cannot do anything halfway. Once you decide to perform, you are the best you can be. You need and want music in your life.

You do need to study philosophy to balance out your aggressive nature. Without spiritual development, you tend to be too material-minded, stubborn, and self-centered, and you strain to attain. You are not a born follower and won't accept organized beliefs without proof. But with study, you will reason it all out and come to your own favorable conclusions.

26/8

This is a very different quality than the 44 or 53. The 2 is sensitive, loves beautiful music and prefers to have things orderly and neat. The 6 is a nurturer that loves children and pets. Six is artistic and has a flair for color combinations. This person knows the law and likes to see it upheld and gets upset when justice isn't served.

44/8

This is the Master Number of the "Master Therapist" or "Great Achiever." The energy put forth by 44s is incredible! They have strong desires and are willing to work hard to achieve them. They will mentally set goals and not stop until they achieve them.

53/8

Five loves and needs freedom. Both 5 and 3 love to travel, not just for enjoyment, but to learn something. With the 8 root these loves will be organized so that all goes smoothly. If this person is in sales, watch out! Nobody could do better. If this person is in sports, again watch out! Nobody can beat him or her.

9 SOUL'S URGE OR DESIRE

The 9 is sometimes called the Mystic Number of Love, for this person exudes a special warmth that others feel. Nines love people and people love 9s. With a 9 Desire, you want to see the good in every situation, the heart of gold in every soul. It represents universal love and compassion for the whole human race, and enjoys being kind and feeling the love in return.

You can be happy for whoever wins the contest, no matter who you are personally pulling for. You realize that the winner needs people to be happy for him or her and there will be another time for the others to have their day of glory. Even if you are involved in the contest and lose, you will show happiness for the winner. Now *that's* a real champ!

Sometimes 9 is called The Great Lover, for 9s are very romantic. You have all the loving qualities of the 3 and 6 that are inside the 9. When you do find the right person, you are a most wonderful and compassionate companion.

Being influenced by the 9 Desire vibration, you love to do nice things for people and hate to see them hurt by anyone else. You will fight for other people's rights and are disgusted with bullies. You would be Superman if you could.

Besides wanting to do good for people, love, and be loved, you do like to travel, meet new people, and share laughter and warmth. With all that you learn, you want to impart that knowledge to benefit others. You are happier giving than receiving, for you get so much more satisfaction in seeing that your gift is really helping someone, or just making them happy.

The 9 vibration is very impressionable. You should never think long about negative things because you feel things so deeply you take in too much sorrow, and that is hard to shake off. You would give your life to save the world.

FROM MY NOTES

This true story may help you analyze a chart. This has to do with a connection between one person's deepest desire and a corresponding Karmic Lesson.

Years ago when I was working on movie sets, I met people of all types, so it was a perfect place for me to evaluate the accuracy of numerology charts. There was one man whom I felt uncomfortable around and didn't know why, until one day he approached me and asked if I would do his chart. Until then we had rarely spoken, and I noticed he hardly talked with people. His friends seemed few and far between. His story unfolded as I read him the meaning of his numbers, and it was most interesting, for it showed me how true a chart can be.

His Soul's Urge was a 3. He also had a missing 3 in his name, his Karmic Lesson. I mentioned this to him, that the very desire he held in his heart was a vibration missing in his name, making it seem impossible to attain. The Karmic Lesson for 3 is that self expression can be very difficult because of a lack of confidence. It is hard to put thoughts into words, and as a result, he may have the feeling that he could not express himself well and may feel shy because of it. Is that true? I asked him.

He said it was true and that he wanted more than anything to be able to speak well, but he felt so inhibited and shy. He went on to say that he had a very unhappy childhood. Never had a birthday party like other kids and, in fact, never got a birthday present. He deeply desired that feeling of being liked and being able to express himself easily.

What number vibration could have been more apropos for this man? The very things he desired were missing from his personal musical scale; and our vibrations do make up our personal musical scale. The Karmic Lessons are the missing notes. But his was not missing completely, for it showed up on one of his strongest areas: in his vowels, his deepest desire. This meant that he would eventually work hard to achieve what was missing in his life.

Also, the fact that his childhood was unhappy fit in with the 3 Karmic Lesson. The 3 represents the child and is a very happy, playful vibration. But the negative aspect of the 3 is just the opposite. Two people can have a 3, and one will reflect the happy positive aspects and another will be just the opposite.

When you read a chart, be sure to scan it well to see where a missing number might be. When you read a chart for someone, all you need to do is tell what his or her numbers mean. You don't have to make up anything. The numbers will tell it all. I had people I barely knew tell me, "You have told me things about myself that even my family doesn't know." And I was as astounded as they were. Numbers don't lie.

Mind/Personality

YOUR CONSONANTS

Your personality is the impression you make—the way you appear to be. What people *think* you are is not always accurate because they tend to judge on what they see. While your vowels are active in your desires that blossom from your Soul's Urge, the sum of your consonants is the real you that not everyone has the privilege to know.

Consonants clothe the vowels and are silent in comparison to the aspirated sound of the vowels. Consonants represent your inner being that is individual in the way you reason and dream, the way you think—the real you when there is no one around to impress, your mind.

Every one of those consonant letters in our name represents a sound that is a part of us that we have responded to all our life, so much so that it is a part of our personality.

Just as consonants clothe the vowels, our thoughts are the substance that clothes us with our expressions. This is shown in our taste in clothing, hairstyle, and personal grooming, the way we dress, and even in our choice of words. All this combined shows in our facial expressions, for our inner thoughts are reflected in our personality and the way that others see us.

1 MIND/PERSONALITY

Are you a 1? If so, you are an original. You think like an executive and run your affairs efficiently. You don't like to be told what to do, but will listen, sift the good from the rest, and make your own choices. You rely on your own decisions because you have faith in yourself. In your work or profession, you are the one who comes up with the ideas. Although you like to start projects, you don't always finish them, so you are willing to leave the details to others.

Appearance

The 1 Personality is quite outstanding and likeable. All 1s appear confident and self-assured, but some of you are powerfully dominant and very persuasive. You picture yourself as a leader and dress accordingly, preferring unique styles that are of your own good taste and sometimes of your own design. You like being a trendsetter. Forget the fashions with designers' names on them; if there is a name on your clothes, it will be your own. At gatherings you will stand out as quite distinguished. Bright, cheerful colors are becoming on you.

Negative 1

Although positive 1s appear dignified and correct, the opposite side of the 1 vibration occurs with the 1s who choose loud, clashing colors and patterns, or are simply untidy. They still are unique in the way they dress, only their taste is more on the wild side, garish, and tasteless. To top that off, they may be overly aggressive, over-bearing, arrogant, dictatorial, pushy, ego-centered, and thoughtless. They are either too daring or just drab in their dress as well as their personality.

2 MIND/PERSONALITY

The 2 desires companionship in personal life and in business. You, with the 2 Mind, want harmonious surroundings and are natural peace-makers to make it so. Because you understand each person's point of view you have a way of being tactful and diplomatic. This innate awareness helps you remain pleasant in an argument. You have a nice way with words and dislike vulgar language. You want people to like you and will do all you can to maintain harmonious relations. You make a wonderful companion. You are sensitive and caring and so nice to be with. You enjoy tending to details and can do minute work with your hands. You also enjoy having collections of your favorite things. Some 2s are very picky about cleanliness and will carry a hanky to clean off a seat in a public place before they sit on it. This tidiness is often true of their wallet as well, with all dollar bills facing the same direction and in numerical order.

Appearance

The 2 Personality is quiet, attractive, gentle, and kind, and stays mainly in the background. You have a pleasant countenance and exude an aura of gentleness, a spirit of caring. You have a natural desire to please people and are generally well-liked, probably because you are a good listener. Some of you don't always have stylish clothes, for you don't want to stand out in a crowd. You are a bit shy and don't care to be the center of attention. If so, you dress simply and in quiet colors. But your clothes are neat and clean and, let's face it, you can be very fussy about every detail.

Negative 2

Unlike the positive 2s that dress conservatively and in good taste, the negative 2s can be quite the opposite: choosing either very plain and colorless attire or flamboyant, showy outfits, or simply unkempt. Those who cultivate an interest in style will ultimately change to classier dress. The negative 2 lacks self-confidence and appears uneasy in a room full of people and tries to remain as invisible as possible. They are very emotional, are super-sensitive, and cry easily. They also display a bad temper and an "acid tongue." A natural urge to collect things can result in an impulse to shoplift. The destructive 2 is a liar, is very sneaky, has shifty eyes, and is not to be trusted.

THE 11/2 MIND/PERSONALITY

The person with this Personality is more attuned to the spiritual, as they know it, than to the material world. If you have the Master Number 11 Mind, you see yourself inspiring other people to have faith and a deeper understanding of life. And you can, for you are filled with idealism and are illumined by a faith of your own. You make friends easily. You do, however, have strong beliefs and may preach to others directly or unconsciously. In other words, you have a bit of the religious leader quality in you. Then again you may be stronger in the creative arts.

You do have many talents and are truly artistic. Your techniques are your own, unusual, and brilliant. Wonderful ideas come to you from the intuitive level during your meditative sojourns in your world of imagination. You really don't care for the business world. Your true fulfillment is found in the ministry or creative arts where you find an outlet for your inventive ability, artistic talents, and original ideas.

Appearance

When people look at you, they see the light of wisdom in your eyes and an electric personality. No doubt they see you as someone special. As a positive 11, you are a source of inspiration and can give people a motivation with purpose. Your clothes show your individual taste, and it's quite likely you may have designed them yourself! You choose to be distinctive and dress with style.

Negative 11/2

Whereas the positive 11 is very attractive with a refined spiritual quality, the negative 11 can be very unattractive)even though handsome or beautiful) because of the inconsiderate, self-centered attitude. Negative 11s will wear loud-patterned clothes, unattractive color combinations, or mismatched items. They can be self-centered, narcissistic, pouty, and inconsiderate, especially if they feel they are not appreciated. They are often frustrated in relationships because no one can live up to their expectations. Some lack the patience of the 2 and pursue destructive means of expression with their creative power. Beware of the one who uses power to rule over others.

3 MIND/PERSONALITY

Joy is the heart of the 3. If this is your number, you are the "Cock-eyed Optimist" who sees the good side of everything. You are the most creative-thinking individual, are quick and witty, have a great sense of humor, and are very articulate. You just love an audience and are happiest when expressing your talents in a way that will uplift, enrich, and entertain them. Of course you would rather play than work so you look for a job or profession that is fun and sociable, or you will make a drab job fun.

Appearance

Personality plus, the 3 is attractive, outgoing, sociable, and popular. People sense your warmth and respond to it and will cluster around you. Your rosy outlook is catchy and you are fun to be with. People find you interesting to listen to, for you express yourself colorfully. Female 3s enjoy wearing jewelry and adding artistic touches to their wardrobe. Men may wear extreme styles, but generally they are known by their friendly nature and for being easy to talk to.

Negative 3

Although the positive 3 has the gift of gab that is fun, there are those who will gossip, be meddlesome, and use hurtful words. They have a tendency to be sloppy, overdo on cheap jewelry, and wear extreme and overly revealing styles. The negative 3 women will be the ones on the block to wear overly revealing clothing and think they are sexy. They have no inhibitions, either. Women wear too much makeup. Some tend to be stoop-shouldered, have bad posture, and be awkward. A dual personality may be present. Unlike the positive 3 with the joi-de-vivre (joy of life) the negative 3 takes life much too seriously to really enjoy it. Many try to avoid responsibility and cannot tolerate criticism, even if it is the good constructive kind.

4 MIND/PERSONALITY

This is the practical and dependable person, a planner who does things in an orderly way. The 4s are our builders who take their work seriously down to the details. In other words, they are honest, reliable achievers. If this is your number, you know the rules and think things out well before applying yourself. Then you take the time to do it right. You may work slowly, but you get results. You are concerned about setting a good foundation for the future and your mind is most always on work. You love your family and have traditional values. There is a deep devotion to your country. You are patriotic in spite of the flaws you see.

Appearance

The 4 influence gives the impression of your being totally self-reliant. You appear straight-laced and conservative; you like tailored clothes for work and well-made sport clothes in plain, subdued colors for casual. You are usually neat and traditional. If you are a woman, you would be very uncomfortable in frills and laces. If you are a man, you aren't attracted to it.

Negative 4

This 4 is either a workaholic or entirely undisciplined. Other negative traits are that they are stingy, overly cautious, lazy, almost afraid to let go and have fun, very plain on purpose, and most often dull and boring. Some are foul-mouthed, have a crude manner, and have a nasty temper, too.

5 MIND/PERSONALITY

This is the most versatile and adaptable person of all! If this is your number, you see yourself traveling all over the world, meeting all types of people, seeing all the interesting historic places. And when you do travel, you avoid guided tours. You will go off on your own and mingle with the populace, try to speak their language and see how they *really* live.

You must, by nature, have liberty to come and go at will. You don't really want responsibility if you see it as inhibiting your freedom. You don't like to be tied down because routine bores you and stifles your imagination. But you can have a happy marriage with the right partner, one who allows you your independence.

You love life and want to try, test, and taste everything. This makes you daring and courageous. Interestingly, the 5 represents the five physical senses, and they are what you must learn to control because it is easy for a 5 to get into bad habits, but difficult for a 5 to break them.

Appearance

Attractive and popular, 5s usually have a sparkling, witty personality and are both versatile and daring. They are good conversationalists because they are eager to learn all they can and always have interesting information to share. With this as your Mind number you can be excellent in sales, for you get along well with most everybody. You can charm people into wanting a product whether they need it or not. You are usually well dressed and can wear bright colors becomingly. Some 5s do wear strange color combinations, though.

Negative 5

Females wear too much make-up and/or are very extreme in their dress. Males, too, are sometimes prone to weirdness of wardrobe— loud colors and crazy patterns. Negative 5s are curious and will try anything once. Cautious? Forget it. They take crazy chances and can be very loud and obnoxious. They are prone to overindulge in sensual things and can be self-destructive. Those who lose control of their physical appetites become alcoholics, drug abusers, chain smokers, sex abusers, or undisciplined gamblers.

6 MIND/PERSONALITY

The 6 is definitely the domestic type. Home and family are important to their happiness. The nurturing instinct is in evidence by the lower circle on the number 6. That represents the stomach area and the womb. The 6 loves good food, has a sweet tooth, and needs to watch the diet. That full tummy can mean too many sweets or a baby for the family.

If you have a 6 Mind, you are artistic and it shows in the special touches you add to your home. You love pleasant music and attractive furnishings, a milieu that represents your idealism and aesthetic appreciation. You also need your own special comfy chair, because you love nothing better than to take off the working clothes and relax in your pajamas and slippers! You enjoy entertaining your friends and make them feel warm and comfortable.

You are a natural humanitarian. You care about your community as well as your family and will take part in projects to better either one of them. Unlike the 9, who worries about the world, you are more concerned for your immediate area and the people you know personally. You are very responsible; you want to pay your bills on time, take care of your young ones and your aging parents, and heal all their wounds. People are drawn to you for advice, and you have a knack for counseling them. You give so much, and all you need in return is to feel appreciated.

Appearance

The 6 influence makes you appear wise and caring, and people are drawn to you for advice. There is a protective, loving aura around you, a fatherly/motherly vibration that gives people a feeling of comfort and security and makes them feel better about themselves. You are happiest in comfortable clothes, so you aren't prone to dressing up. You may be overweight because of your love of food and desire for sweets.

Negative 6

The truly negative 6 appears slovenly and careless in dress and demeanor. Some are so certain they are always right that they interfere in other people's business and tell them what they should do. Some tend to express their love in a smothery way, not realizing how overbearing they are. Others are bad housekeepers, untidy, and careless. They can be self-righteous, smug, or obstinate, and domestic tyranny is not uncommon.

42/6

The 4 must have security and is willing to work hard for it. The 2 is very sensitive and takes everything to heart.

33

This Master Number is the vibration of *spiritual giving*. If you have the 33/6, you give a great deal of yourself in acts of kindness. You are sensitive to others' heartaches and do all you can to alleviate sorrow. You have consideration for all life; you are kind to animals and feel for their plight. You love children and see them as blossoming souls capable of expressing the best within them when guided properly. The 33 vibration in you influences you to give freely without thought of reward, for your joy is in the giving itself.

Appearance

The 33 makes you appear unpretentious, gentle, and kind. Your manner is always appropriate and cultured.

Negative 33

They can be so sympathetic as to deny their own needs. They are martyrs.

7 MIND/PERSONALITY

Seven is the thinker, the educator, the philosopher, and the scientist. This is an analytical mind that wants to know why and will investigate to uncover truths. If this is your mind number, you adore libraries and large beautiful offices with many books. Being a nature lover, you dream of panoramic windows that look out over a gorgeous view. You would rather spend time alone with a good book than chatter idly with anyone. But good conversation in select company of mature, intellectual like-minded persons who have depth and quality is appealing to you.

The 7 in you loves a quiet, peaceful atmosphere and draws you to the country or other uninhabited spot where you can get happily lost in deep thought in your own dream world. You are so intuitive you find it easy to slip into the alpha consciousness where you hear that inner voice that guides you. Sometimes you get answers in dreams. You are mystical. Then there are those 7s who don't believe in mysticism, but in cold scientific facts. They too are intuitive, but don't know it.

Appearance

As a 7, you stand out from the crowd. You have a certain dignity and a feeling of mystery about you that is very attractive. You can be cold and aloof, but when you know and like someone you open up and become the most interesting talker, for the 7 in you searches for facts and knows things that most people don't even think about. So you are respected for your knowledge. You are happiest being well-groomed and neat. Your clothes are usually conservative and in good taste.

Negative 7

If the 7 avoids philosophy and the spiritual, it becomes frustrated, depressed, introverted, and unfriendly. Some of the negative traits are: antisocial, nervous, crude, fearful, suspicious, and unreasonable. Whereas the positive 7s are dignified and impeccable dressers, the negative 7s are the opposite: careless, woebegone, and unapproachable. Some would just as soon become hermits and live in the woods.

8 MIND/PERSONALITY

Eight is a mental number, meaning this person is about ideas, not physical labor. So if you have this Mind number, you are a natural executive and cannot be happy in a subordinate position for long. It is best for you to be the boss or own your own business. Good judgment and organizational skills are inherent in this vibration. You are the money-maker and you earn every cent you make. The 8 Mind appreciates and works best in plush, successful-looking surroundings. You desire power, wealth, social privilege, and control. Your mind is so active and full of ideas and ambition that you no longer finish one project when you start another. Some 8s make fine athletes and do well in sports. Others are wonderful musicians. Music is a latent talent in you and you may discover enjoyment in it later on in life.

Appearance

The 8 influence gives you a strong, physical body and radiant good health. Your personality is very upbeat, positive, and even dynamic with a touch of flamboyance. There is an air of authority about you, and you are persuasive and genial. You dress well, preferring a few select expensive clothes to a closet full of cheaper duds, so you do look prosperous.

Negative 8

The negative 8 will misuse its power to put people in bondage. Truly destructive 8s use their power for inflicting cruelty and they will retaliate in evil ways. They enjoy flashing large wads of bills to impress all the *little* people. They are loud and they sulk.

17/8

The 8 brings out the good judgment and fine upbringing as well as athletic ability and good health. The 7 gives you distinction, setting you apart from others. Either you look as though you have more money than you do, or your friends never suspect you have as much as you do have because you don't flaunt it.

44/8

This is a Master Number that means "strong on earth." It is called "The Master Therapist" because 44s solve the material needs of the world. If the 44 makes up your 8, you have great strength of conviction, knowing exactly what needs to be done. You will tackle any problem confidently. You are well disciplined because you have incredible mental control. Your accomplishments benefit many individuals. The 44 makes a super counselor. Edgar Cayce was one such person, and his Birth Path was a 44. Dr. Jack Ensign Addington of the Abundant Living Foundation also had the 44 Birth Path, and he gave spiritual insight, hope, and rehabilitation to countless prisoners and others through his radio ministry, "Peace, Poise and Power," for many years until his death in the mid-1990s. Wherever that 44 appears in your chart, it bestows great strength for good.

Appearance

A 44/8 definitely looks like a leader. People sense your special gifts and trust them to guide you to where they should be.

Negative 44

You are over-worked from lack of balance between work and play. Those who ignore the spiritual aspect become frustrated and completely off kilter.

9 MIND/PERSONALITY

Are you a 9? If so, you want with all your heart to see happiness and harmony and to help the world attain it. Your compassion is such that you understand people's suffering and want to alleviate all of it. You are emotional and it is easy for you to put yourself in anyone's situation and sense exactly what he or she is going through. You make the most convincing actors for this reason. A mere thought can produce a tear.

The 9 influence is romantic. You long for personal love, but will sacrifice it in order to help others, for you love to be of service and counsel. You care for and comfort others. When you personally experience losses and sorrow, you are able to pull yourself up and go on attaining success again and again. You want to create something of lasting beauty and have the talent for doing so. You give selflessly to causes you believe in.

People sense your compassion and truly love you. Everyone loves a 9 for the 9 is kind, charming, warm, outgoing, and courteous. You always make a favorable impression because of your innate personal magnetism.

Appearance

You want to be comfortable and casual, but well dressed when it comes to formal occasions. The 9 influence tends to help you look young well into your senior years, especially if you keep your good posture and wear lighter colors. You even feel better in lighter colors and intuitively stay away from blacks and browns.

Negative 9

Although the positive 9 is warm, compassionate, and loving, the negative 9 is a self-serving, insensitive egoist. You don't just dress casually, but carelessly. Other negative traits are being possessive, impulsive, moody, careless with money, and fearful. Over-emotion can rob you of your energy and you end up depressed and bitter. Truly negative 9s crave attention, are narrow-minded, will use power for personal gain, and spend money foolishly and then need it. The destructive 9s are apt to be violent.

18/9

You are very active and good health is important. You want to exercise, eat the right foods, and stay physically fit. Some of you have the gift to heal. You are inclined to dream vivid, detailed dreams and have a remarkable imagination.

27/9

This is a successful business vibration. The 2 has the desire to help others, and the 7 has the intellect and the wisdom to do it.

The Total Expression

VOWELS AND CONSONANTS

Together, the vibrations of the vowels and consonants in the Birth Name reveal the reason why we are here. The Total Expression, or simply, Expression, is the number of our *Destiny* and includes all of our talents and potential. It tells us what we must do; it's a guide to how we can handle our Birth Path by showing us where to look for opportunity. When our talents are channeled to the right vocation we find our greatest fulfillment.

1: LEADER/DECISION-MAKER

If your full name comes to a 1, this means you are not a natural follower. You like to do things *your* way, and you most often do, for you have the will and the determination. Your ideas are original so you are destined to lead. In order to be happy in your career, you must select a job where you have the opportunity to work your way up to the position of boss, manager, or the one in charge.

You have an inventive mind that helps you solve problems before anyone else. You have the courage, creativity, and vision that set you apart from others. You find that if you want anything done properly you must do it yourself, particularly the main issues. You prefer to leave details to others. You like to start things but not necessarily finish them.

It is built in you to not want to lean on anyone else, so until you mature you will have many experiences that will teach you to use your will and determination as tools for success. If you follow your natural impulse to stand on your own, you could become a most outstanding person in your community—or in the world.

All 1s should read Dale Carnegie's *How to Win Friends and Influence People*. All need to cultivate friends and appreciate them.

Negative 1

Bullies. Loners. Bossy. Impatient. Impulsive. Boastful. Aggressive. Very selfish. Over-inflated egos. Use their power for evil purposes.

Occupations

Business owner. Director. Manager. Inventor. Lawyer.

In the creative arts: Writer. Designer. Artist.

10/1

All the above, plus 10s are old souls who have the ability to bring people together for a common goal. Most 10s are spiritual. Negative 10s are closed-minded and opinionated.

19/1

Nineteen is known as the *love vibration,* for it attracts love and money. If this is your number, the 1 gives you will and determination; the 9 will orient you more toward public service. You are dramatic, so you make fine actors and motivational speakers. Negative 19s appear to be what they are not. They look positive on the outside but can still be very negative people.

Nineteen is one of the four Testing Numbers (13, 14, 16, 19). Whenever you see these numbers, immediately think *caution,* there is a lesson to be learned here, a test to be passed. The 9 represents humanity and caring about people. The test is for the 1 to learn that *you reap what you sow.*

2: THE PEACEMAKER

Ah, the 2. You have a gentle nature and a lot of charm. In this world of rudeness and disrespect, you are thoughtful and courteous, two traits that make people feel warmly about you. You are a natural companion, enjoy partnerships, and should always work with or for others. You are cooperative, and patient and very good at details. You discover that you don't want or need to be the center of attention but are happiest working quietly in the background where you can be appreciated for the work you do so well. And you do need to know that you are appreciated.

The 2 influence gives you an inborn desire for peace and harmony. Coupling that with your tactful ways and ability to see both sides of an issue make you a natural diplomat. But this same ability makes it difficult for you to make your own decisions. You can feel another person's joy or pain and are pretty emotional yourself.

You hate to travel very far because you are a homebody who loves your home, garden, and flowers. If you are to be happy, you should have a job or profession that keeps you close to home.

Negative 2

Overly sensitive. Cry easily. Hurtful words cause pain. Rely too much on people. Fears being alone. Selfish. Stubborn. Bossy. Sneaky. Convincing liars. Thieves. Ruthless thugs.

Occupations

Detail workers. Jewelry makers. Watch repairers. Composers. Musicians. Mechanics. Repairmen. Bookkeepers. Librarians. Analysts. Astronomers. Physicists. Teachers. Landscapers. Gardeners. Sculptors. Diplomats. Counselors. Publishers. Artists. Dancer in groups. Merchants. Waitresses and Waiters. Civil servants. Companions. Homemakers.

11/2

The 11 is refined, almost elegant. If your name comes to the Master Number 11, it is hard for you to keep your feet on earth for you are such a dreamer, so highly intuitive, that the world of imagination is very real to you. You desire to enlighten others to truths, as you know them. You have definite leadership tendencies (the double 1). Many 11s attain fame in the arts: music, acting, painting, teaching. Others achieve success in ministry. Then there are those who never realize their full potential and work mainly in the root of the 11, which is the 2, staying mainly in the background. But the true, positive 11 is dedicated to spiritual and/or artistic fulfillment.

Negative 11

Ideals so high no one can live up to them, so many remain frustrated in personal life relationships. Use power for evil purposes.

20/2

The cipher (0) always represents God-power that intensifies the vibrations of the root number. If 20 is your full name number, you are more sensitive, more emotional, and more understanding than any other. You also are faced with many more decisions in life. Your emotions are intense, but if and when you learn to manage them you gain mastery over your life and feel more in control.

Negative 20

Fear death (*death* also vibrates to 20). Kleptomania.

Note: Any negative use of any vibration causes a negative reaction to anything else of the same vibratory rate, and 20 can make you edgy and ill at ease.

3: THE ENTERTAINER

If you have a vibrant personality that stands out in a crowd, chances are your Birth Name comes to a 3. You are probably quite attractive, too. You have a great deal of enthusiasm, optimism, and a good sense of humor. If you aren't the entertainer, you should write the script, for 3 is full of creative ideas and has a fully developed funny bone and a gift for words. You are the happiest in any job where you can be creative. You may be the one who performs center stage in a life of applause. You have a part to play in the drama or in a business that uplifts people and lightens their burdens. And you do have the *gift of gab*.

There are those of you who use this gift to inspire, enrich, and uplift people as a performer, the writer of the script, or anywhere else you can use your self-expression to bring joy to others. Your talents should reward you well monetarily.

Of course, you will have times when you feel down. We all do. But you can train your mind to be optimistic and to expect the best. What we feel, we attract. That is spiritual law. And no one seems to sense this more than the 3.

Negative 3

Gossips. Take life too seriously or not serious enough. Whine and complain. Irresponsible. Extra sensitive. Easily hurt. Careless about details. Very emotional. Lacks self-control. Burdened. Deceitful. Intolerant. Jealous.

Note: The 3 tends to scatter its energies. See how open-ended the 3 is compared with the 8? Sound silly? Well, the symbol is drawn to reflect what the vibration is about, and 8s focus their attention on what needs to be done, whereas 3s need to learn to focus on one thing at a time until it works.

Occupations

Writer or performer. Speaker. Poet. Actor. Musician. Singer. Dancer. Entertainer. Artist. Decorator. Jeweler. Commerce. Business. Society leader. Welfare worker. Critic. Clergyman. Literature.

12/3

If your full name reduces first to a 12, you have an inherent poise and inner harmony. You understand people and aren't upset if they don't conform to your own ideals. Once you gain spiritual insight, you can see clearly how you cause your own problems and are able to deal with them effectively by changing your attitude. If the name starts with the letter L (12th letter), you are blessed with a beautiful singing voice.

21/3

If your name reduces first to 21, you are very expressive. Success comes easy because of your talents and positive outlook. You are born writers. You desire to express yourself in the arts and are flawless with details. Good fortune is meant to be yours.

30/3

If your name reduces first to 30, you usually have a happy disposition, love children, and stay younger-looking longer than most people. If the name starts with an L (12th letter of the Hebrew alphabet but numbered as 30) you are blessed with a beautiful singing voice and possibly are a natural writer. You have many artistic talents and have skills in communication.

48/12/3

If your name reduces first to a 48, you seek satisfaction and find material success. You are a loyal supporter of home, family, and country. You take things seriously and, though you have a good sense of humor, you wonder why some people laugh at things you don't find funny at all, especially if it is hurtful to someone.

4: THE PLANNER/WORKER

We're glad we have you 4s. You are the genuine producers in this world! You are a talented manager for the 3s who have the talent of expression but not the managerial capabilities. You are the born organizer who wants a secure foundation and will build slowly for the future. You want to do things correctly step-by-step. It all requires work, but you are disciplined because you know you will have something worthwhile to show for it. The results of your labor must be seen if you are to feel you have made an accomplishment. Fours enjoy detailed work (2+2) and will patiently take one step at a time in order to achieve perfection. You take your work seriously and get things done. You cannot tolerate those who goof off on the job because you feel work should be taken seriously.

You are good with your hands. Many 4s are mechanically inclined. Others are musicians and artists. You are all generally honest, hard-working people.

Honesty and integrity are a part of 4's nature. People know you are reliable and can count on you. You are square solid citizens, usually moral, and often dull—not dull in your personality, but because of being such a workaholic.

Negative 4

Over-worked (forgets to relax and have a little fun too). Critical. Straight-laced. Opinionated. Moody. Extremely cruel (because of deep-seated hatred.) Antagonistic. Vulgar.

Occupations

Builder. Mason. Contractor. Physician. Surgeon. Buyer. Economist. Architect. Electrician. Plumber. Dentist. Tailor/Seamstress. Waitress/Waiter. Farmer. Gardner. Mechanic. Shoe repairer. Technical writer. Author. Printer. Financier. Musician. Scientist. Accountant. Chemist. Engraver. Draftsman. Landscaper.

13/4

Thirteen is one of the four Testing Numbers (13, 14, 16, 19). The test is for the 1 to remain focused and complete the work that is to be done. The danger is to slide back into an unenthusiastic and lazy attitude where nothing is accomplished. The test, then, is to be dedicated to completing something worthwhile.

Negative 13

Over-indulgence. Addiction. Insecurity. Frustration.

Note: Owning a home relieves some frustration and insecurity.

22/4

This is a Master Number known as The Master Architect, for people with this vibration achieve great things. If your full name is 22 and you set a goal, you usually attain it, for you find ways of accomplishing things that no one else would even think of, and you do nothing halfway. You have a purpose and a plan, appear to be in control, and are looked up to as the expert. You put your ideas into concrete form to benefit as many people as possible. Waterways, roads, dams, and skyscrapers are examples of such ideas.

Negative 22

Robbers. Safe-crackers. Sly and underhanded in business.

Note: This is such a strong vibration that the negative side is destructive and evil. Jails are full of misdirected 22 energies. It is imperative for them to learn to be responsible citizens.

Occupations

Builder. Shipper. Buyer. Casting director. Architectural engineer. Efficiency expert. Director of world affairs. Translator. Creative writer. Designer. Certified Public Accountant. Lawyer. Surgeon.

5: THE TESTER/TASTER

Basically, 5s are seekers of freedom and knowledge and are really curious people. If this is your full name number, you want to know what makes things tick and what is going on. You will investigate anything. You love the freedom to come and go as you please. You need a change of scene and are very uncomfortable in an office of four walls sitting at a desk all day (just the opposite of the 4s, who appreciate established routine). But give you a job where you can travel, and come and go as you please, and you will succeed beyond belief. Fives are born salespeople. Why, you are so outgoing and charming and get along so well with most people that you can sell anything by your enthusiasm alone!

That 5 influence makes you love to travel and gain the knowledge that comes with it. Your natural curiosity has you digging for facts. You are intellectual, versatile, energetic, progressive, and adaptable. Not only that, but you have a nice personality and charm, and you are a good conversationalist, too. You don't mind the crowds at all. You are a people person!

The 5 symbol is drawn open-ended and on a rocker to depict all these traits: open-ended to show the outgoing nature and loving to talk, the rocker showing movement to represent travel and change, and the 5 itself representing the five physical senses to enjoy to the fullest. Let's face it: you love change and welcome new opportunities. And yes, you even like to exercise!

Negative 5

Restless. Discontented. Moody. Impulsive. Impatient. Outspoken. Bad-tempered. Rude and profane. Gambling excites them and they will take crazy chances that often become their downfall. Debauchery. Perversion. Drug use. Alcohol.

Occupations

Salesperson. Real estate broker. Athlete. Musician. Dancer. Performer. Writer. Journalist. Columnist. Advertising. Publicity. Stunt person. Racer. Artist. Scientist. Translator. Investigator. Archaeologist. Tour Guide.

14/5

Fourteen is one of the four Testing Numbers (13, 14, 16, 19). The 5 root represents change and freedom. The test is for the 1 to learn to become adaptable, not bound in like the 4, and to use its freedom wisely. The 5 has the urge to overdo in its physical appetites. But the power of thought is there, for 14 is composed of two 7s, the vibration of mental perception and analytical ability, which are inherent aids to overcome temptations.

23/5

The 2 gives the ability to see both points of view. The 3 gives creative expression through its writing or speaking talents. Together they make the 5 adept in communicating ideas. People like you because you are complimentary and use your tact to make people feel good.

6: THE NURTURER/COMFORTER

Thank heaven for 6s. You are the world's teachers and healers. This domestic vibration, known as the Cosmic Parent, appreciates home and family and loves beautiful surroundings, peace, and comfort. If this is your full name number, you understand the law and innately know what is right. You are not argumentative. Instead, you will sit and rock and nod pleasantly as someone spouts off and, when all the frustration has been vented, you will gently steer the person around to right thinking. Sixes make fine counselors and advisors because of this ability.

The 6 influence makes you sensible, trustworthy, and mature. You should look for a career that engages your positive qualities that include your artistic abilities, good management, speaking well, understanding law, being a fine judge of character, and having insight into personal problems. All 6s need a position of responsibility, for they are the natural humanitarians with self-respect and high ideals who desire to heal all wounds and right all wrongs.

Many of you go into the medical profession or become veterinarians. There are those of you who cannot bear to witness sickness, but vibrate instead to the artistic side of the vibration. You have a good feel for color, decorating, and art. Six is the voice in the career, so here we find teachers, professors, speakers, orators, and media personalities. Many go into politics to help the community or just be on the board of directors so they can have the power to help where it is needed. Some become the president of their organization or a nation.

Negative 6

Smug and conceited. (Often feel that no one else is competent enough to do the job as well as they can.) Outspoken. Self-righteous. Meddlesome. Stubborn. Worries a lot. Need constant appreciation. Anxious. Revengeful. Jealous. Domestic tyranny.

Note: Domestic tyranny happens because of jealousy, mistrust, or not being able to make someone believe or behave the way 6s expect.

Occupations

Doctor. Surgeon. Nurse. Childcare provider. Caregiver. Veterinarian. Artist. Painter. Landscaper. Decorator. Singer. Speaker. Orator. Radio and television personality. Teacher. Professor. Lawyer. Politician. Community leader.

15/6

They have the same qualities as previously discussed, but with more ambition. The 1 being the strongest influence shows they will promote themselves first. If this is your full name number, you like the things the world has to offer (5) and are willing to go after your desires. Whereas negative 15s step on toes to get ahead, positive 15s get there through mental ingenuity. You must learn to deal with your intense feelings.

33

This is the Master Number of spiritual/selfless giving. Same as above, but representing more loving service, compassion, and deep understanding. You are gentle, kind, and unpretentious, have a nurturing instinct, and give with no thought of return. You are an earth angel. The negative 33 mopes and whines and is often the martyr.

7: THE THINKER/EDUCATOR

Technical advances would suffer if it were not for the 7. If this is your full name number, you are naturally philosophical, for you think so deeply about things. Wonderful ideas come to you in daydreams. There is a quiet dignity about you: reserved, graceful, poised, aristocratic, refined, and spiritual. You love nature and quiet places, and you can be alone and not be lonely. Yet you may fear loneliness.

The 7 influence makes you intellectual, intuitive, and secretive. You speak only when you have something to say, and then you are most interesting because you are a font of knowledge on the subjects you have studied. A library is a must for you because you must have books on hand to round out your thoughts and supply answers to your profound questions. You love soft music for the inner response you feel from it, and something stirs inside you from the right poetry. You may not realize it, but you have such keen perception that you can almost see another person's thoughts. All 7s have this ability to a greater or lesser degree. You often remember your dreams, and you usually dream in color.

As a symbol, the 7 is drawn to turn its back on the numbers 8 and 9 that follow it, for they represent the future. Seven is the number of rest, thoughtful consideration, and study, and it appears to reflect on the numbers 1–6 before it. This shows its interest in the past, whether it be personal or that of history. So you just may be an avid collector of historical pieces and antiques. Or maybe you are the 7 with the great memory.

The 7 cannot divide itself. It therefore prefers to work alone or be over subordinates. Is this true of you? The 7 is a perfectionist. It truly enjoys research. This means you like to specialize and will study and train hard to become the most knowledgeable and expert in your field.

Sevens are either scientific or spiritual; a few can be both. With the 7 influence, you are a seeker of truth. You are eclectic where religion is concerned, for you refuse to accept anything on blind faith. Those who are spiritual make fine clergymen for they have depth of thought and are analytical, cautious, observant, and utterly charming.

Negative 7

Ulterior motives. Sarcastic. Suspicious. Schemers. Argumentative. Unreasonable. Either talk too much or not at all: glib or reticent. Self-centered. Sneaky. Dishonest. Abusive. Cruel. Malice of forethought. Convincing liars.

Note: They don't mind becoming hermits because they prefer being alone. If married and stray, they will justify their being unfaithful.

Occupations

Authority on religions and churches. Minister. Educator. Scientist. Investigator. Mathematician. Astronomer. Inventor. Judge. Lawmaker. Attorney. Editor. Writer. Watchmaker. Weaver. Librarian. Lecturer.

16/7

The same qualities as previously discussed, plus 16 is one of the four Testing Numbers (13, 14, 16, 19). The root 7 represents faith and spirituality. The 6 is the body, for Adam was created on the sixth day, and every body has six sides in our three-dimensional world: front and back, top and bottom, right and left. The 6 equates with physical love and procreation. In this lifetime or one before, there may have been physical abuse or children born out of wedlock. The test is for the 1 to seek the spirituality of the 7 in order to balance out past karma and avoid ruination that comes from strictly material living.

Sixteens have a love for words. They express themselves creatively in writing and speaking. Those who want more in life will find meditation most satisfying. Striving only for riches will make you feel as though something is missing—spirituality is missing.

25/7

This 7 is more adventurous than the others due to the curiosity of both the 2 and 5 and the 5's desire for freedom to explore and learn. If 25 is your full name number, you will come up with unusual solutions. This is due to your love of detail. You are very sensitive but never let your emotions show. All 7s are very reserved, and all have meaningful dreams.

43/7

If 4 and 3 are the numbers behind the 7 root of your full name, you have a strong sense of justice. (The honest and reliable 4 comes first.) You are quite dignified and have leadership ability. You are a true friend and very tolerant. Because of your keen intuitive perception, you think things out clearly. You accumulate facts and present them in an interesting manner. These talents are valuable to you as a writer, teacher, and lecturer.

8: THE EXECUTIVE/JUDGE

Many successful businesspeople, musicians, and athletes have achieved their success due to the influence of the 8. You are meant to succeed and make a lot of money.

If your full name is an 8, you have inborn skills for organization and management. You are meant to hone those skills so you can be an authority in your line of work or profession; otherwise you will always feel frustrated. With 8 as an influence you can put your ideas to practical use, giving you a natural executive ability and excellence in business. This does not always mean it will be easy. It means you will achieve through personal effort, and that will bring you much success. With this Destiny number, you should be in a position of authority, a star athlete, or a popular performer.

The 8 is the only number that you can draw over and over without lifting your pencil. Because of this, it has become a symbol of eternity This is also a symbol of stamina and continual energy. Many athletes will have this as a destiny number or in their Physical Plane of Expression for in it there is energy, enthusiasm, and physical stamina. Eight refers to money (or the lack of it) because money itself is really energy. Don't you notice how little energy you have when your bank account is low?

It is interesting to know that the 8 was originally drawn to represent two worlds: the spiritual and the physical, one above the other. And the influence of this vibration is that the energy of both worlds is necessary for complete success. In other words, you will do better in life if you have some spiritual knowledge to aid you in mastering yourself while you are developing your natural skills for your profession.

Philosophers have likened the 8 to a double mirror, windows, or eyeglasses, because its influence helps one to see both sides clearly. With this ability comes good judgment. Eights have a feeling for what is successful and how to manage money. They make good doctors, for they see the overall picture. Rarely do they specialize because they would rather treat the whole person.

A good sense of rhythm is inherent in this vibration, so many musicians have this Destiny number. Some discover their latent musical talent in later years.

Negative 8

Financial problems. Impatient. Tense. Selfish. Intolerant. Materialistic. Ruthless. Oppressive. Violent temper. Drug users. Alcoholics.

Note: There is a great need for them to balance themselves by studying philosophy. They want so desperately to look rich that they will spend beyond their means to create the look of having achieved it all, or stoop to marry for money rather than love, thinking that will fill their gap of desire.

Occupations

Business person. Banker. Broker. Financier. Athlete. Musician. Band/Orchestra leader. Commerce expert. Ship and railroad business. Engineer. Politician. Doctor. Manufacturer. Supervisor. Director. Judge. Literary Field.

17/8

All the previously discussed, plus the 7 brings out the desire to probe into things, to study, research, and seek out the truth. It brings insight and intuition. This is the person who does the thinking and prefers to work alone. The 1 is independent in nature, the one with the original ideas.

26/8

The 2 brings in the desire for partnership, interaction with others where communication is essential, and has the gift to keep harmony by knowing how to handle others with tact. The 6 brings in extra ability to speak well and communicate effectively. Both number vibrations have interest in business partnership, marriage, home, and family. Negative 26s must learn to control their tempers and impulses and to not be preachy and controlling.

44/8

This is the Master Number of the Master Therapist. This Destiny is to better the world in a personal, practical way. With the double 4 preceding the 8, they are very logical and resourceful. They can take spiritual concepts and put them to material benefit by helping people build or rebuild their lives. Here we find the super counselors, advisors, ministers, and doctors. Negative 44s appear to be tense and often feel limited. Destructive 44s have as great a potential for evil as fine people have for doing good.

53/8

When the 5 comes first, there is more assertiveness required in order to attain the goal. Five wants answers and will look for them. Three takes the results and, if packageable, makes them attractive. Five likes facts and 3 writes them down. Both 5 and 3 are numbers of movement and travel.

9: THE HUMANITARIAN

With this warm, outgoing personality and dramatic flair, the 9 always makes a favorable impression. If this is your full name number, you most likely practice the high ideals you find so attractive and want to use them to inspire others to those heights. You hate to see anyone suffer, and, if you are able to show people how to alleviate their stress and problems, you will do so because you really do care. You will teach, act, heal, advise, and create beautiful things in order to raise the consciousness of the world.

Because you are emotional, you can identify with all kinds of people and understand those qualities in them. This is the trait that makes 9s such outstanding actors. And your tendency to daydream makes you the most sensitive of artists. You are a perfectionist, and no matter what work you choose you demand the very best from yourself. You are loving, charitable, compassionate, forgiving, virtuous, patient, and tolerant, and you give selfless service.

The top circle on the 9 represents the keen mind filled with the wisdom of the lessons learned in numbers 1 through 8. (Every number exists in the 9.) To be so highly evolved means there will be many trying times, tests to go through, ordeals, and trials. Life isn't always easy for you, for you are born to be of service to others. Nine is *the finishing number*, the tying up of loose ends, putting to test all of the accumulated wisdom and then inspiring others to learn it from you. Once you learn forgiveness and to express compassion, life is very good and rewards you in many loving ways.

Negative 9

Self-serving. Egotistical. Possessive. Impulsive. Moody. Shy. Restless. Insensitive. Compulsive shopper. Impressionable. Destructive tendencies. Squanders money.

Note: All 9s are very impressionable. It is best for them to stay away from habit-forming drugs and dangerous influences found in graphically violent movies.

Occupations

Healer. Doctor. Surgeon. Philanthropist. Humanitarian. Teacher. Beautician. Receptionist. Aviator. Judge. Advisor. Criminal lawyer. Spiritual leader. Astronomer. Lecturer. Entertainer. Humorist. Actor. Writer. Publisher. Composer.

18/9

All of the previously mentioned, plus the 8 is a vibration of strength, so good health is important. You will want to exercise, eat the right foods, and stay physically fit. You are inclined to dream vivid, detailed dreams. You have a remarkable imagination and intuition. You strive to complete your projects because the influence of 9 is to finish what you begin.

27/9

This is a successful business vibration. You with the 29 full name number possess the intellect and wisdom (7) to help others with sensitivity toward their needs (2) that together give you the ability to accomplish much good.

FROM MY NOTES

When you have the opportunity to read charts for many people, as I did in my days on movie sets, you will have one eureka after another when reading for people and getting their feedback on what you tell them about their numbers. There was one very attractive man who seemed to be working on every upscale set in the business. I saw so many 8s in John's chart that I told him he should have been a banker. "Oh, I was, for many years in Florida. Then I got so tired of it that I decided to take a leave of absence and come to California," he told me.

He went on to say that he was running out of money and wrote home for some to return on. While waiting, he went to see a stage production of *Hello Dolly*. After the show, he met one of the dancers, who told him that with his good looks he should go to Los Angeles first, register at Central Casting, and get a few jobs as an extra so he could earn the money of his own. So he did just that, and one of his first movies was *Easy Come, Easy Go* starring Elvis Presley.

Elvis asked John if he was a member of SAG. "No," John told him, "but I would like to be." At that Elvis walked over to the producer, and as he spoke he pointed out John and the producer nodded. Then to his delight, John was given a line to say to Elvis. Immediately after he filmed, Elvis had one of his friends take John to SAG so he could join. John never returned to Florida but worked happily in movies from then on. Here was a man with many 8s in his name and chart, being helped by Elvis, who was born on the 8th of the month. That was a numerical vibration they had in common and, because of it, they immediately felt some sort of bond.

Your Birth Path

The Birth Path shows what you are here to do.

This is found in your birth date: month, day, and year added and reduced to its root number. First write the number of your birth month, followed by the day and the year. For example, November 12, 1979 = 11/12/1979.

1. January	**5. May**	**9. September**
2. February	**6. June**	**10. October**
3. March	**7. July**	**11. November**
4. April	**8. August**	**12. December**

Next, add each of the month, day, and year down to its root:

Month: 11 = 2

Day: 12 = 3

Year: 1979 = 26 = 8

Now add those root numbers 2 + 3 + 8 = 13. 1 + 3 = 4.

4 is the Birth Path.

If the 13 were a Master Number, such as 11, 22, 33, or 44, it would not be reduced.

Hint!

When I figure the Birth Path, I write it this way for clarity on the chart: 11/12/1979 = 31/**4**. And yes, you may take the 19 of the 1979 and use it as a 1, because 9 + 1= 10, and 1 + 0= 1. It is quicker to add the year this way: 179= 17= 8. We get the same root to add to the month and day, *but* by adding 10 instead of the root of 1, you may find a Master Number otherwise missed, so best to check each way.

The Birth **Day**, exclusive of the month and year, is the "real you" at maturity. Using Chart 4, be sure to read all about your Day number(s). If it is a double number, such as 12, you add those two numbers to find the root (1+2=3). So 3 is the root, and the 1 and 2 are the adjectives that describe that root even further. So read about all three numbers to understand the real you at maturity.

BIRTH PATH 1

You are here to learn independence and self-reliance. Natural executive abilities are part of your make-up, so you are likely to be a leader in the field you choose. You have original ideas and like to get them started, but prefer to leave the details and finishing to someone else so you can go ahead with your next idea.

You dislike being bossed around. You can see a better way of doing things and prefer to do them your own way, so you will seek work where you can be promoted and eventually be in charge or go into business for yourself. Remember: You will always be responsible for your own actions, and you must learn self-control.

Your opportunities are realized more quickly when you hone your special abilities of perception and concentration. By creating more practical methods, you make yourself invaluable where you work and show your leadership ability while remaining cooperative and positive in attitude. You have innate skills in design and illustration, in writing and speaking. You could find a niche in the government, medicine, the arts, entertaining, and business of all types.

Some Well-Known People With a 1 Birth Path

Susan B. Anthony. Carol Burnett. Truman Capote. Jacques Cousteau. Charlie Chaplin. Sammy Davis, Jr. Walt Disney. L. Ron Hubbard. Placido Domingo. Mikhail Gorbachev. Billy Graham. Janis Joplin. Martin Luther King, Jr. George Lucas. Steve Martin. Michelle

Pfeiffer. Ralph Nader. Jack Nicholson. Napoleon. Florence Nightengale. Robert Redford. Jean Renoir. Dr. Seuss. O. J. Simpson. Bruce Springsteen. Leo Tolstoy. Spencer Tracy. Sarah Vaughn. George Washington.

BIRTH PATH 2

Yours is a path of service, to work in cooperation *with* or *for* others. The 2 is a kind and cooperative vibration filled with sensitivity. Those of you with this path create a calm atmosphere wherever you happen to be.

You are neat and orderly. Your sensitivity is so strong that you are hard on yourself when you make a mistake. In other words, you are a perfectionist and accurate down to the detail. You work easily with small objects, so many of you become jewelers, artists, musicians, or any profession that requires patient work with the hands.

You have a need to know that your work is appreciated, so you are more comfortable when you work with others rather than alone. Because of your powers of persuasion, tact, and diplomacy, you are a natural peacemaker. You have the knack for organizing, negotiating, assisting, and supporting our country's leaders. You do have to learn to be a better listener and talk less, but most of all overcome your sensitivities and learn to control your emotions. No one has control over your happiness but you.

You will find your opportunities where there is a need for fine, detailed work, in diplomatic relations, in any of the arts, writing, speaking, drama, the ministry, or in dealing with finance. You also find much success in partnerships.

Some Well-Known People With a 2 Birth Path

Julie Andrews. Richard Burton. Piper Laurie. Norman Mailer. Eduoard Manet. Claude Monet. Sidney Poitier. Ronald Reagan. Debbie Reynolds. Robert Louis Stevenson. Dr. Benjamin Spock. Gloria Vanderbilt.

BIRTH PATH 3

You are at your best in creative, artistic, or intellectual careers. It is important for you to focus on one favored talent and specialize in it, for it would be so easy for you to become a "jack-of-all-trades" and never settle into a dependable job.

The 3 influence gives you the gift of words, so you are a great communicator. You are able to write the script or be the actor performing it. Yours is a bubbling personality that lifts people's spirits, so you are sociable and popular. It takes a lot to get you down, but when that happens just rest awhile to recharge your figurative batteries and soon you are bubbling all over again. You have the gift of gab and your optimism is catchy.

You hate practical or routine work because it limits your freedom. You want your work to be fun, a life of enjoyment and making others smile. Because of this, you are happiest employed in any of the creative fields where you can use your inspirational talents of writing, teaching, performing, lecturing, acting, designing, and so forth. Many 3s attain a position of authority once they understand the rules and practice discipline.

There is a sensitive side to your nature for 3 is an emotional vibration. There will be times when you feel hurt and will want to withdraw into yourself to just be quiet and alone. On the other hand, you can be quite critical of others. Just realize that they too can be sensitive to criticism. All in all, you are blessed with a lot of talent and a quick wit, and you are most often a pleasure to be with. You are attractive, too.

Your opportunities lie in the creative fields, literature, marketing, and business, but best of all in careers that amuse and entertain: arts and crafts, teaching children, and inspiring people in general with your cheerfulness and friendly ways.

Some Well-Known People With a 3 Birth Path

Hans Christian Andersen. Louis Armstrong. Ethel Barrymore. Yul Bryner. Maria Callas. Frank Capra. Eldridge Cleaver. Bill Cosby. Bing Crosby. Billy Crystal. Salvadore Dali. Ella Fitzgerald. Jodie Foster. Judy Garland. Helen Hayes. Alfred Hitchcock. Andrew Jackson. Robert F. Kennedy. Ann Landers. Norman Lear. Vivien Leigh. Olivia Newton-John. Walter Pidgeon. Joan Rivers. Margaret Mead. John Ritter. Sugar Ray Robinson. Barbara Walters. John Wayne.

BIRTH PATH 4

You are here for accomplishment through work. The 4 Birth Path is the one where you must follow an organized process in order to achieve your goals and attain security. There is no shortcut on this path. You are here to learn to take things patiently, step-by-step. You are given the talents to do so, being a born organizer, very practical, and having the desire to do things exactly right in order to secure a firm foundation for your future. Plus, you want to see something substantial for your time and effort.

All 4s are good with their hands, but with different talents. Some are mechanically inclined. Others are musicians, and others are artistic in color and design. The 4 has no time for the abstract, flights of fancy, or the dream world. Make it manifest here and now by working tirelessly toward a goal; that's what appeals to the 4.

You need time for fun and relaxation, but the 4 influence makes you too serious, and you feel guilty taking time for it. So you must work on lightening up your load and being more cheerful. You can be very stubborn and set in your ways, so you must learn to give and take, live and let live. Yet the good qualities shine through. You are honest and reliable, dependable, persevering, exacting, and patriotic, and you look forward to coming home to your family. You are happiest and most productive when you can work at your own pace without someone telling you what to do. In fact, you hate being told what to do. You will do things your own way anyway.

Your fields of opportunity lie in building, buying and selling, management, real estate, educational and administrative lines, repairing, machinists, music and performance, dealing with documents and contracts, paperwork, and in general, providing the public with necessities.

Some Well-Known People With a 4 Birth Path

Nat King Cole. Marie Curie. Sigmund Freud. Robert Frost. Elliott Gould. Hugh Hefner. Henri Matisse. Paul McCartney. Grandma Moses. Dolly Parton. Will Rogers. Babe Ruth. Carl Sandburg. Jim Thorpe.

BIRTH PATH 5

You are here to learn through experience, to appreciate the value of freedom and the right use of it, and in the gathering of information. You are quite independent and very active, for you have a lot of energy to use creatively. No matter what type of work you settle on, you must have a creative outlet in recreation or a hobby. If not, frustration will get the best of you.

You love your freedom and cannot tolerate being fenced in by time (nine-to-five jobs), places (desk jobs), or by heavy responsibilities that rob you of that freedom. You happen to be born with an innate dislike for routine, so you should never tie yourself down to that kind of work. Yet you do have a sense of reliability. And knowledge? Yes! You want to know a lot about everything. You have an insatiable curiosity and you want to know what is going on around you and in the world. In this new age, the Internet beckons you with all its information. You enjoy analyzing what you discover.

The 5 energy loves to travel and mingle with people. You have a penchant for learning other languages, adapting to new surroundings, and experiencing all the varieties that life has to offer. After all, 5 does stand for man and his physical five senses that are easily tempted, and man must learn self-control. (Man has five extremities: two arms, two legs, and a head to direct them.) Fives are fun, popular, and full of enthusiasm. They are our daring heroes, too. They enjoy a risk.

The 5's field of opportunity lies in any line of work where there is change and variety. They are people persons and are best in any work dealing with the public: selling, sports, stunts, acting, performance, music, art, politics, real estate, investments, legal matters, and business in general where they aren't stuck at a desk for long. Some are attracted to the occult or to science.

Some Well-Known People With a 5 Birth Path

Lauren Bacall. Harry Belafonte. Irving Berling. Victor Borge. Marlon Brando. Johnny Carson. Walter Cronkite. Charles Darwin. William Faulkner. Benjamin Franklin. Clark Gable. Helen Keller. Billie Jean King. Abraham Lincoln. Walter Matthau. Sir Isaac Newton. Rudolf Nureyev. Theodore Roosevelt. Franklin Delano Roosevelt. Bertrand Russell. John Steinbeck. Lily Tomlin. Vincent Van Gogh. Denzel Washington. Tennessee Williams.

BIRTH PATH 6

This is the love, domestic, artistic, and humanitarian vibration. If this is your path, you are here to find pleasure in responsibility and in service to others. You are definitely the marrying type, though some 6s don't marry at all for fear of being hurt. This *is* an emotional and sensitive vibration. You have a strong desire for home and family, for you love children and make a good parent. In fact, the 6 is known as *the Cosmic Parent.* You love animals too and may have several pets. Plants may adorn your home and gardening would give you much pleasure.

There is a fatherly/motherly aura about those of you with this Birth Path. People are drawn to you for advice. You feel the responsibility and help as much as you are able. The 6 influence makes you a fine counselor. Just think about it and you know that you know how to comfort and soothe those who come to you.

The 6 influence is responsible for your high ideals, artistic sense, and longing for beautiful surroundings, so you can be sure your home is attractive and comfortable. You must have your own personal easy chair. Because of your love for beauty in all types of artistic mediums, including paintings and sculpture, decorating, designing, and so forth, you have a natural feel for color combinations.

Some 6s are drawn to nursing and medicine, for they find happiness in alleviating pain. Others are drawn to science, local community projects, or politics on a wider scale in government, for they have a strong sense for what is right and want to do their part in achieving those ends.

As any of these, you need to understand where to draw the line when it comes to giving of yourself or you may become bitter and resentful. You must learn to allow your family members to make their own decisions and learn from their own mistakes. Truly negative 6s are control freaks and watch every move too closely for their loved ones to be comfortable. The negative 6 would rather do everything and do it right than to take a chance of someone else fouling up, and this can cause resentments. You have to learn to let go and trust those close to you.

Fields of opportunity are found in areas where you can make life easier for people, comfort them, beautify their surroundings, or entertain them. You find your niche in medicine, politics, writing, story-telling, photography, singing, dancing, music, invention, ministry, science, engineering, religion, education.

Some Well-Known People With a 6 Birth Path

Elizabeth Barrett Browning. Mikhail Baryshnikov. Dale Carnegie. Lewis Carroll. Carlos Castaneda. Agatha Christie. Christopher

Columbus. Joan of Arc. Albert Einstein. King Richard III. Jascha Heifetz. Isaac Asimov. Stephen King. Fred Astaire. Cary Grant. David Niven. Phil Donahue. Thomas Edison. Jesse Jackson. D.H. Lawrence. John Lennon. Joanne Woodward. Michael Jackson. John McEnroe. Linda Ronstadt. Beverly Sills. Meryl Streep. Steven Spielberg. Pope Paul VI. J. R. R. Tolkien. H. G. Wells.

BIRTH PATH 7

If this is your Birth Path, you are here to gather wisdom. You are the thinker, an idealist who is selective, analytical, scientific, and usually quiet, secretive, and reserved. Because of the 7 vibration's love of study and searching out facts you can be the most interesting of talkers. People look up to you because you appear wise and knowledgeable. And no wonder, the 7 influence makes you happiest in a lovely library surrounded by your favorite books where you have access to all you desire to learn.

Sevens are either coldly scientific or warmly spiritual, so you are interested in material facts or in philosophical thought. Either way, you need to spend time away from the crowds and noisy places that jar and upset your inner psyche. You are most comfortable surrounded by the beauty of nature where you can meditate on the deeper meaning of life. It is your dream to live in the country away from the city noise and pollution.

You must have a mate you respect or you would rather be alone. Yet you fear you will be alone because it is difficult to meet someone who lives up to your expectations. When you do meet that special someone, you can be the most loving and giving mate to that person.

Because of the 7s' academic interests they make fine teachers, detectives, criminal investigators, ministers, lawgivers, judges, doctors, writers, scientists, astronomers, mathematicians, educators, and those in radio, television, and movies.

Some Well-Known People With a 7 Birth Path

Bella Abzug. Arthur Ashe. Edwin "Buzz" Aldrin. Joan Baez. Candice Bergen. Leonard Bernstein. Helen Gurley Brown. William F. Buckley, Jr. Sir Richard Burton. Frederic Chopin. Eric Clapton. Fyodor Dostoyevski. Michael Douglas. Carrie Fisher. Mel Gibson. Woody Guthrie. J. Edgar Hoover. Vladimir Horowitz. Chet Huntley. John Fitzgerald Kennedy. Golda Meir. Marilyn Monroe. Mary Tyler

Moore. Gertrude Stein. James Stewart. Harry S. Truman. Rudolph Valentino. Robert Wagner.

BIRTH PATH 8

You are the executive type and came here to excel in your chosen line of work and be very successful. The 8 is an ambitious achiever who has the endurance to follow through, a natural executive who is able to lead others in large endeavors. You are born with good judgment and have the natural ability to inspire people to greater attainments, so you make an excellent boss.

The 8 is a material number that influences you to strive for and think of making money, but you are happiest when you find the spiritual balance along with your material gains. So it is wise for you to study philosophy. But you must understand the laws regarding money or you could be in need of it. Wealth will either come easily or there will be stress and strain to attain.

Opportunities come most often through prominent people. The 8 Birth Path is most often involved with large organizations and corporations. Your field of endeavor could be in business, banking, writing, editing, printing, publishing, sports, athletic activities, acting, music as a soloist or conductor, pipe organist, lawyer, judge, historian, politician, archaeology, statistics, and government.

Some Well-Known People With an 8 Birth Path

Muhammad Ali. Lucille Ball. James Baldwin. Melvin Belli. Ingrid Bergman. James Cagney. Edgar Cayce. Caesar Chavez. Jack Dempsey. Bob Dylan. Mary Baker Eddy. Millard Fillmore. Roberta Flack. Timothy Leary. Jack London. Mickey Mantle. Groucho Marx. Lisa Minnelli. Bob Newhart. Paul Newman. Jack Nicklaus. Sir Laurence Olivier. Jesse Owens. Norman Vincent Peale. Mary Pickford. Oliver Stone. Barbara Streisand. Adlai Stevenson. Elizabeth Taylor. Johnny Weismuller. Brigham Young.

BIRTH PATH 9

The 9 came into this world with a lot of wisdom, and its influence will have you spend your life helping to raise the consciousness of humanity, for you are a natural giver of good. You give without thought of reward and are forgiving. You have such high ideals, are so romantic, and love so deeply that you make a wonderful marriage partner. You are passionate, giving, and understanding. You expect as much of other people too, and are often disappointed in most people because of their lack of idealism, social graces, and other finer qualities.

The 9 influence makes you very dramatic and gives you a flair for living. You prefer to find beauty everywhere and are very disappointed when this is not always so. You will do your best to continue to help, counsel, and try to raise the average person to a greater height of understanding.

You are deeply moved by beautiful music, and you love all of the creative arts. Love is especially important to you for you have deep feelings and are very sensitive to other people's feelings as well. Too much aloneness brings on frustration. You find the greatest happiness in giving selfless service. Your innate sensitivities are responsible for helping you to become great as an actor, for you are able to get *inside* a character's personality and become one with it, which is detrimental at the same time if you portray someone very vicious.

All kinds of opportunities come to you through artistic and inspirational people and in just about any and every vocation: the arts, education, literature, religion, government, and charities. They say a 9 loves everybody, and everybody loves a 9.

Some Well-Known People With a 9 Birth Path

Louisa May Alcott. Francis Bacon. Tallulah Bankhead. Bridget Bardot. Walter Brennan. Jimmy Carter. Ray Charles. Harrison Ford. Mahatma Ghandi. Julia Child. Samuel Goldwyn. Benny Goodman. Jean Harlow. Richard Harris. Jimi Hendrix. Dustin Hoffman. Whitney Houston. Ernest Hemingway. Carl Jung. Burt Lancaster. Charles Lindbergh. Clare Boothe Luce. Shirley MacLaine. Annie Oakley. Cole Porter. Elvis Presley. Richard Pryor. Colonel Harlan Sanders. Albert Schweitzer. Bishop Fulton J. Sheen. Mark Spitz. Gloria Steinman. Patrick Swayze. William Howard Taft. Henry David Thoreau. Lawrence Welk. Orson Welles. Walter Winchell.

BIRTH PATH 11

The 11, known as The Psychic Master, is a strong vibration for inspiring ideas and using creative forces. It is more spiritual in its composition than the 2. There is a certain light about you that separates you from the crowd. To be born on an 11 Birth Path means you are here to inspire others to achieve their full potential. You have a way of motivating people to do better and they look to you for encouragement and to lead the way, for you have that spark of wisdom in your eyes and know how to say the right words at the right time. As does the 2 root, you have innate tact and diplomacy that you use to preserve peace and harmony about you. Anything new in science or in religion appeals to you, so many ministers and counselors have this Birth Path.

Artists, musicians, actors, and public speakers also have the sensitivity of this 11 vibration. Your intuition is strong and you are creative, original, and inventive. You have the desire to learn all you can and are likely to achieve fame in your line of work, some of you with a partner. You have an artistic temperament, are musical, and want to lift the hearts and thoughts of people with your talent, be it art, writing, speaking, singing abilities, in performance (solo or as a duo), or in the ministry. That is where your opportunities lie, and you are apt to achieve great fame as long as you stay true to your calling. Finding a partner who can live up to your standards is very difficult. Some 11s become renown for setting bad examples.

Some well-known people with an 11 Birth Path

Dame Judith Anderson. Kevin Bacon. Lionel Barrymore. Jack Benny. Al Capp. Marc Chagall. Bill Clinton. Peggy Fleming. J. Paul Getty. Goethe. Bob Hope. Doug Henning. Harry Houdini. Madonna. Mozart. Jacqueline Kennedy Onassis. Henry Kissinger, Edward R. Murrow. Edgar Allan Poe. Jules Verne.

BIRTH PATH 22

This is the vibration known as the *Master Architect,* for people who have this Birth Path have made such major accomplishments on such a large scale. They are truly the material masters, for the 22 is where we find the builders of great buildings, roadways, and musical instruments, fantastic inventors, writers of renown, great statesmen, musicians, executives, and leaders who are dynamic, organized, and practical.

If yours is a 22 Birth Path, you have the drive and the desire to make your dreams a reality. You accomplish much through cooperation and particular attention to detail. You are blessed with strong, analytical perception, and your clear thinking helps you set and outline your goals the way no one else can. Yes, you may encounter failures that frustrate you, but what you learn from them perfects your final plan—if you don't get aggravated over the whole thing and give up. And you must watch your health. Your brainpower dwarfs your physical stamina.

The field of opportunity is the world! The 22 accomplishes any large endeavor that does the most for the most people.

Some Well-Known People With a 22-Birth Path

Woody Allen. P. T. Barnum. Annie Besant. Samuel Clemens (Mark Twain). James Michener. Luciano Pavrotti. John D. Rockefeller III. J. D. Salinger. Frank Sinatra. Margaret Thatcher. Oprah Winfrey.

BIRTH PATH 33

This is the energy of *selfless giving*. The occupations may be the same as the 6, but the way the work is handled will be on a higher level of sensitivity. If this is your path, you work more toward perfection and impose very high standards for you to live up to. The 6 root represents the voice in the career. When elevated to the 33 vibration we find at its height the great orator who stirs men's souls, the great teacher who makes an everlasting impression.

The 6 is the vibration of love, family, service, and responsibility. But the 33 is much more sensitive to the needs of others, so you will feel their hurts and sorrows as deeply as your own. You often won't show it emotionally, but rather remain noticeably cool while you do all in your power to alleviate stress and pain. It is known as the love vibration in its highest form: compassion.

Some Well-Known People With a 33 Birth Path

Fred Astaire. Mikhail Baryshnikov. President George W. Bush. Dale Carnegie. Agatha Christie. Albert Einstein. Stephen King. D. H. Lawrence. John McEnroe. Linda Ronstadt. Beverly Sills. Steven Spielberg. Meryl Streep. H. G. Wells.

Chart 4:
Birth Day Chart

Much can be told about you by your Birth DAY alone. People who share the same day numbers have been found to have a lot in common, regardless of the month or year. And, what they *do* have in common corresponds to the numbers of their Birth DAY. That number represents *YOU* at maturity.

A person with a single digit Birthday, such as the 7th, would express all the attributes of the seven. Those who have a double-digit Birthday, such as the 25th, would express not only the root of 7, but the adjective numbers 2 and 5 as well. For your Birthday, see the attributes related to your number(s) on the following chart. There are positive (+) and negative (-) traits to consider.

	+	**-**
1	You are a leader with executive ability and administrative talents. Traits that give you great potential for success are your independence and originality, determination, self-confidence, ambition. Your excellent mind is filled with creative ideas, and your strong will-power. You love to start projects and have others complete them so you can go on to the next project. You have strong likes and dislikes, don't follow fads because of preferring to be unique. You are a doer rather than a watcher. You are quite outstanding.	The opposite of the positive 1: lacks initiative, is lazy and boastful, and loves self above all. Self-conscious. Stubborn. Selfish. Braggart. Egotist. Bully. Repressed feelings. Easily bored. Very upset if they can't follow their own beliefs. They hate to be told what to do and wont hesitate to cause trouble.
2	A follower, you prefer not to be the one to make the decisions, and are happy to accompany others wherever they want to go. You have a nice personality, are sensitive to others' feelings, and are friendly, tactful, affectionate, diplomatic, helpful, cooperative, considerate, charming, loving, and work well with others. You make a good companion or partner. You are a good partner for a 1 because you are better at continuing projects than starting them. You love to be home, and there you have collections of your favorite things. You like things kept in order, neat, and clean.	Occasional moods of depression. Easily offended. Dissatisfied. Over-emotional. Bad temper. Fastidious to a point of fault. Follower. Shy. Careless. Sneaky. Liar. Coward. Cruel. Thief.
3	You are so expressive. Many of your special qualities are that you are talented, cheerful, outgoing, and optimistic. You have a delightful sense of humor, and wit, too. You love to make people happy. As a host, you are the best, for you are sociable, charming, enthusiastic, and quite the entertainer. You enjoy singing, and the arts. You have the artistic touch. Your exceptional imagination makes you good at writing and speaking. You always have something to say. Cheerful colors appeal to you. You enjoy traveling, especially long distance.	A gossip. Talks too much. Vain. Jealous. Wasteful. Critical of others. Scatters energies. A worry-wart. Bored. Dislikes responsibility. Hates work unless it is fun. Doesn't take life seriously. Too much makeup. Extreme styles.

	+	-
4	All 4s are practical. You are a good worker, organized, accurate, conscientious, conservative, committed, sensible, reliable, and patient. People appreciate you for your enthusiasm and know you are responsible and helpful. You appreciate family and country are loyal, sincere, and patriotic. You are disciplined and like to see that trait in others. You want the law enforced. You prefer the tailored look and hate frills.	Opinionated. Headstrong. Argumentative. Too serious. Intolerant. Prejudiced. Narrow-minded. Dull. Over-worked. Jealous. Crude. Vulgar. Strong negative emotions. Bad temper. Must see to believe. Not affectionately demonstrable. Too busy to simply relax and enjoy. Inhibited.
5	You are charming, witty, popular, and attractive to the opposite sex. You have a quick mind, are adaptable, versatile, and enthusiastic. You are curious, analytical, entertaining, energetic, and very affectionate. You love to travel for you have a love of freedom and new experiences and adapt easily. You make a super salesman, for you are dynamic and progressive as well as social and enjoy working with people. Some of you are extreme in dress.You are courageous and not afraid to try new things.	Over-indulge in sensual things: alcohol, food, sex, and drugs. Perversion. Careless. Rude. Crude. Irresponsible. Restless. Impatient. Impulsive. Gambler. Takes dangerous chances.
6	You are a true friend. People come to you for advice, healing, comfort, and sympathy. You are just, honorable, protective, and very responsible. You are domestic. You adore your home and family and are a devoted parent. You are creative and artistic, and like your favorite colors and artwork in your home. You look your best when you are out, but at home you dress comfortably. Your are affectionate, poised, generous, understanding, harmonious, and have high ideals and standards. You give loving service, and are good at finishing things. You are lawful and want to see the law upheld. You use your voice in career: teaching, singing, speaking, counseling, the healing arts, or politics.	Needs to feel appreciated. Self-righteous. Smug. Interfering. False pride. Anxiety. Meddlesome. Cynical. Self-centered. Jealous. Suspicious. Domineering. Bossy. Expects too much of people. Child abuser. Sex offender.
7	You stand out from the crowd as dignified, wise, and silent. You are a nature- and book-lover. It is important to you to be knowledgeable. You are analytical, and either religious with a great deal of faith, or agnostic. You are scientific. You have a good mind, great inner strength, are poised, peaceful, refined, logical, intuitive, and a perfectionist. Many great teachers and professors have this 7 vibration. You love history and antiques. You have elegant taste in clothes and feel best when dressed well.	Cold and aloof. Unapproachable. Sloppy. Sarcastic. Fearful. Sly. Chit-chatty. Gossip. Cheat. Secretive. Deceitful. Broods. Lives in the past. Represses emotions. Stubborn. Hermit/loner. Mean. Abusive. Critical of others.

	+	-
8	You like to look your best, wear the finest materials, wear sucessful-looking clothes. You want and should be the one in charge for you very capable, have executive ability; are able to see the whole picture and work well with people. You are goal-oriented, self-confident, efficient, ambitious, dependable, practical, and have good judgment. Some are athletic, due to healthy, stamina, and balanced energies. If not involved with music now, you do have latent musical abilities. You are a moneymaker and good with money. You find unique solutions to problems.	Needs to look prosperous. Will marry for money. Impatient. A schemer. Pushy. Thoughtless. Materialistic. Intolerant. Temper. Needs philosophical study. Not frugal. Abusive. Raw.
9	You have a magnetic personality and get along well with everyone. You are warm, loving, romantic, compassionate, empathetic, full of brotherly love, regardless of race or religion. People are people and deserve kindness. You have artistic abilities and good sense of color. You are an inspirational. Idealistic. Strong will power. Logical. Boundless imagination. Have creative solutions. You are broadminded, unselfish, philanthropic. You are quite an actor—very dramatic yet sincere. You dress classy yet comfortably.	Highly impressionable. Over-emotional. Frustrated. Unfulfilled. Burdened. Aimless. Immoral. Liar. Vulgar. Bad habits. Dissipation. Addiction. Morose.
11	You are a dreamer of great dreams. You can teach and enlighten people and inspire them to great achievement. Many of you become religious leaders, as you have high ideals and are interested the spiritual, religious, and/or the occult, and like to explore the unknown. As such you are dramatic and persuasive. Your other qualities are that you are inventive, intuitive, inspired, and very aware. You have what it takes to be a great artist in music, art, or drama.	Sets goals too high to reach and then gets frustrated. Fanatical. Aimless. Dishonest. Miserly. Wants power to control. A wicked leader.
22	You are a master achiever and capable of leading large organizations. It is your desire to build something of value for the most people: buildings, roads, bridges, musical instruments, etc. While the 11 builds dreams, the 22 makes them a reality. You are able to manifest from grand ideas, for you are a sincere hard worker who is so good at details. You are powerful. You are a peacemaker.	Narrow. Uncultured. Inferiority complex. Ulterior motives. Restless. Wicked. Gang leaders. Black magic. Super sensitive both emotionally and to the touch. The negative side of this vibration is that of the accomplished safecracker. There are more incarcerated people with this misused energy than any other.

Inner Guidance

The Inner Guidance Number is the frequency we tune to when we go about solving our problems.

It is well known that our brain waves emit frequencies during our thinking process. In our waking moments, they emit beta waves and in sleep they are delta. In that time between wake and sleep, a state of meditation, they are in the alpha frequency, which is the borderline between conscious and unconscious activity that precedes sleep.

When we work on our problems consciously, we are in the beta state. But when we relax and go into the calmness of meditation for problem solving we reach the alpha state, where we have access to our Higher Self for answers. Our Inner Guidance Number pinpoints our personal use of these energies that help us decide how to handle problems.

Our Higher Self vibrates at twice the rate of our personal expression, so to find your Inner Guidance Number, you either double your total name number (Total Expression or Destiny) or add that total name number to the vowel and consonant numbers. Check both ways, for one may give a Master Number that would otherwise be missed (see Chapter 2).

Following are the Inner Guidance Number vibrations and the problem-solving meditation for each. This is the same number vibration but holds a clearer answer because we are open to hear our inner counsel. Each ray is a state of consciousness, and we can use it for effective meditation.

10/1 INDEPENDENCE AND ORIGINALITY

You solve your problems yourself. You know your own abilities and trust your own judgement.

Negative 1

Every decision is entirely selfish. May be aggressively impulsive.

First Ray Meditation: Will

Concentrate on one desire or problem at a time. Seek the Will of your Higher Self and you will be directed to the great center from which all ideas originate. When you tune into this first ray, your awareness is raised, perception is keen, and all options are clear.

2 SENSITIVITY AND COOPERATION

You don't always trust your decisions because of your talent for seeing both sides of a question. You will often go to others for advice and then decide. But when you do decide, you make sure every detail is considered.

Negative 2

You are too pessimistic to think clearly. It is too difficult to make your own decisions so you lean on others.

Second Ray Meditation: Wisdom

Meditate first on Wisdom. This is the area of pure intellect. Your Higher Self is in tune with this ray, and by meditation you become one with this active force. By keeping your goal in view you will see, with your inner eye, the result of any conscious action. This will enable you to make the wisest choices for the action you will take.

3 COMMUNICATION AND SOCIABILITY

You don't always take your problems seriously, for you have an optimistic outlook. You come up with creative solutions and you enjoy discussing them. You are enthusiastic.

Negative 3

Too self-centered. Scatters energies. Worries and frets. Has lack of direction. Talks more than thinks.

Third Ray Meditation: Understanding

Seek Understanding. In meditation your Higher Self connects you with insight into any problem. Leave behind any preconceived opinions and be open to truth and true purpose. and you will become aligned with it. The right answer comes clothed in a feeling of peace, a sense of knowing. Understanding makes the way clear for you.

4 PERSISTENCE AND DEDICATION

Unlike the 3, you take your problems seriously, face them squarely, and work them out in an organized way. You handle them with honesty and expect honesty in return.

Negative 4

Too serious, argumentative, and stubborn. Unwilling to bend because of set opinions. You think you are right at all costs.

Fourth Ray Meditation: Mercy and Gentleness

This is a ray of manifestation that wants to make your desires into reality. In meditation, it is reached with deep humility and honesty and by desiring an answer that is fulfilling and due us by divine right. Having an attitude of kindness and gentleness lightens our load, lessens our stress, and gives us a brighter outlook. This attracts peaceful solutions, which are the balanced center of Mercy.

5 TESTER AND TASTER

You are willing to try different solutions and are not afraid to take chances. You often learn through experience. You will gather much information in order to make the right decision.

Negative 5

Too restless to take time to apply self. Will procrastinate. Can be totally irresponsible and thoughtless until emotionally mature.

Fifth Ray Meditation: Severity

This fifth ray is not as harsh as it sounds. It is a protective force that helps us maintain our balance by setting up boundaries for direction. Remain detached from the problem. View it impersonally, coolly, and calmly. Ask for Divine Order and meditate on right process so that the actual steps you must take will be revealed. Then firmly follow through each step with the feeling of the fifth ray's strength behind you. It is disciplined action.

6 COMMITMENT AND IDEALISM

You are very concerned; you want to take the responsibility and do it right. You consider the feelings of your family and others close to you. You will nurture and protect.

Negative 6

Inclined to meddle in others' affairs. Can be smug and self-righteous. Controlling. In own problems can be obstinate and slow. Will worry and complain.

Sixth Ray Meditation: Beauty

Approach meditation in a state of joy and it will connect you with the sixth ray of Beauty, the ray of the Christ-consciousness whose reflection is in the solar plexus within us all. This is the ray that holds every true answer. Love and beauty are the route to satisfying every need. Any problem can be solved in a loving way. This is a state of consciousness that radiates beauty of expression and right, loving action. When we call on Beauty, we are one with peace and reap peaceful solutions.

7 FAITH IN SELF AND INSIGHT

You analyze the facts and work out your own solutions. You wouldn't dream of asking for someone else's advice. Answers often come through meditation, through books, and from within you.

Negative 7

Suspicious and unreasonable. May have hidden motives—even consider cheating to get results. Will find fault with everything and thereby find it difficult to make a rational decision.

Seventh Ray Meditation: Victory

Approach meditation in the consciousness of having already accomplished the goal in spirit, and ask for the proper physical steps to fulfill it. Have a pencil and paper handy to list the steps received by your Higher Self, which is the seventh ray of Victory. Let the energy of the word Victory fill you with a feeling of accomplishment through Divine Order. When we focus on our goal in meditation, we are given the steps and the courage to follow through to Victory.

8 ORGANIZATION AND JUDGMENT

You have innate good judgment and can formulate your own plans. If unsure, you will pay for expert advice.

Negative 8

Will strain for material things. Can be overly ambitious with motives for self-gratification. Will not consider others' feelings; on a power trip. Tension will cause overreaction. Desires money; needs to look prosperous.

Eighth Ray Meditation: Glory

To enter this eighth ray, we meditate on the glorious feeling that comes with self-respect and knowing that those with whom we associate also respect us. With this sense of self worth we reach up to our Higher Self, which is in tune with this eighth ray of Glory, and present our desire or problem in the spirit of "feeling good about it," and knowing we are worthy of fulfillment. Then we must see ourselves as having the talent to bring it about in all its perfection and glory. When we approach a problem with self-confidence, that energy field of self-worth is sensed and respected by others.

9 COMPASSIONATE AND EMOTIONAL

You won't do anything that will hurt anyone, so your decisions take other people's feelings into consideration.

Negative 9

Wants to please everybody in order to look good. Easily depressed. Held back by daydreaming rather than deciding and doing. Becomes too emotional to think straight.

Ninth Ray Meditation: Foundation

Foundation is in the fourth dimension where our desires take form before being clothed in matter. Whatever we meditate on and see clearly with our mind's eye is where our answers take form in the silence. To reach your ninth ray, breathe slowly in and out until you find that center of strength and poise within you. Meditate on balancing those energies on a firm foundation of strength. As you consider your desire or problem, know that you have the foundation of intelligent reaction to opposition and the self-control to handle any resistance.

Keep your eye on your goal and feel as though it were now a reality. Bathe that reality with your calm inner strength and with a sense of peace and acceptance. See the details that unfold during your step-by-step process for fulfillment. Realize that the strength of that peaceful energy will be with you as you physically take the steps toward accomplishing your goal, and the stability of the firm foundation will remain with you.

It is said that in the circle, 1 and 10 meet, only on a higher level. To realize the answers to problems and to achieve desires, we must tune into the energy field of supply, which is brought about more quickly by working through all ten rays where they find perfect manifestation in 10.

1. Exercising will.
2. Wise choice.
3. Insight and understanding.
4. Gentleness.
5. Discipline.
6. Joyful expectation.
7. Seeing victorious completion.
8. Feeling worthy of it.
9. Balance energies; stand firm.
10. See it through to perfection.

11/2 INTUITIVE AND INSPIRED

You are very intuitive and will often rely on hunches and inspiration.

Negative 11

Can be very dishonest. Thinks only of self and what can be attained. Completely lacks understanding. Loses through carelessness, apathy, or timidity.

Meditation: Second Ray

See page 87 for second ray meditation.

22/4 BRILLIANCE AND INGENUITY

You are a master of accomplishment. You can figure out solutions when no one else can. You check the fine print and catch details that others miss. You have much nervous energy until you solve your problems.

Negative 22

Cunning and underhanded. Can plan detailed schemes for self-attainment. Not to be trusted.

Meditation: Fourth Ray

See page 88 for fourth ray meditation
Reduce master numbers 33 and higher to 1–9.

Your Golden Goal

There comes a time in life when we wonder what our golden years will be like. We don't think about it much when we are young, for it seems so very far off. Usually when we reach middle age, we start to analyze in what direction we are headed and realize it is not too soon to start planning for our hopefully carefree days of retirement.

Some people find that their greatest achievements are still ahead of them. New challenges loom ahead and new ideas fire them up with excitement and a new fortune may be won. People with this feeling and attitude experience a wonderful longevity along with their success, for they have enthusiasm that keeps them forever young.

Fullness of age should mean fullness of life and enjoyment, not retirement from life with a gradual depletion of energies, as is so often expected. To finally settle down and satisfy that something within them can lead to the most fulfilling time of their lives.

Sometimes it takes some serious thought to get deep enough within to really find that core of desire. But it IS deep within each and every one of us.

Every child has fantasies. If you could go back in time into that child-mind you once had, you might remember some of your inner-most dreams. Therein you may find the key to your *Golden Goal*.

There is a rate of vibration to that inner dream, and a number can be put to it to reveal it to you. The clue to your final fulfillment is found by adding your Total Expression (full name number) to the number of your Birth Path. This combines the total YOU with your

93

talents and reason for being here. Together they add up to your
GOLDEN GOAL!

Your name number   ___
Your Birth Path   + ___
Total   = ___   **= Your Golden Goal**

1 Golden Goal

You will have the chance to do all the things you have thought
about for years. You are very independent and you are also very set in
your ways, and that could affect your success. But your original ideas
and inventive ways of seeing them through to fruition can lead to a
most fulfilling time of your life.

2 Golden Goal

You will enjoy hobbies and collecting things. People come to you for
advice, and there may be situations where you find yourself being the
peacemaker. This is a time when you can get involved in artistic pursuits
such as drawing, painting, dancing, music, and going to museums and
libraries. You will enjoy associating with others. Due to increased sensitivity, you either become more easily hurt or more spiritually aware.

3 Golden Goal

You have many talents longing to be expressed, and you are at
your best when you are entertaining others. You find creative outlets
through the spoken or written word, so this is the time to write that
book. Any creative interest will blossom now and there is opportunity
for a rich, full life, perhaps greater now than ever realized before—if
energies are not wasted. This is a good retirement number and there
will be chances for pleasant long distance travel.

4 Golden Goal

You aren't one to sit in a rocking chair and watch the world go by.
You will always find work to do and the opportunity to accomplish
many things. You will plan and organize things of interest to you. The
foundation you lay could be of benefit to others. Your interests may
be in religion or science. Or you may be a musician who will continue
to enjoy performing your music. You will find fulfillment through
your accomplishments.

5 Golden Goal

Senior years will be bustling with activity, travels, and/or diverse amusements. Let go of the old and welcome the new. Your newfound freedom to come and go as you please will prove to be exciting and fulfilling. You may travel more, learn new things, even write and lecture, as you will be most fluent with words.

6 Golden Goal

This is a good retirement number, and this could be a most satisfying period in your life. You will settle down, and if you are single, there is a good chance you will find that right someone and marry. There will be responsibilities, such as caring for the aged or the young, or perhaps finding happiness in just doing some good for others. You could accomplish more than you expect and have financial reward for your services, especially if performed cheerfully and without thinking just of yourself. If an artist, you may teach your craft and/or produce some of your finest work.

7 Golden Goal

You seek to enjoy your time alone with your thoughts, books, and select friends. You will be delving into philosophy and pursuing other mental interests, and you may fulfill an urge to write. There is a good chance you will be called on to teach. Imparting your knowledge to others may prove to be most rewarding. You will want to retire, to be away from city crowds. The natural beauty of unspoiled country appeals to you. But don't be a hermit or you will not find the *joy* that comes from enlightening the few who come to you.

8 Golden Goal

Great success can come to you in later life, maybe fame and fortune. There will be opportunities to supervise, maybe counsel. You will have the chance to use your executive abilities and good judgement in a most satisfying way. Philosophical things will interest you if they have not before. You now have the time as well as the strength and stamina to attain your personal goals.

9 Golden Goal

In later years you will find joy in helping others. It may be through philanthropy, writing, lecturing, or teaching, or in the medical field. It could very likely be in performing. You will enjoy the arts, to attend or to perform. Anything that will uplift humanity will give you pleasure, for you will find your happiness lies in service to others, and there will be both personal and financial reward.

11 Golden Goal

The true mission of Master Numbers is in ministration to many people. The vibrational frequency of 11, the Psychic Master, makes you intuitive and sensitive, enabling you to draw answers from a higher realm. You can inspire others with your high ideals. If you love to be such an inspiration, this can out-picture in religious ministering. Or opportunities may present themselves for you to achieve your goals through any of the communications media. Your inventive and intuitive powers will be at their height.

22 Golden Goal

This is an extremely potent vibration. When you enter this period of time there will be a great opportunity for you to realize your highest achievements. You can succeed as a world leader in important movements if a foundation has been set for it earlier in life. If not, accomplishment on a much bigger scale than ever before in your life is possible now. In some cases the individual prefers to follow the base path of the 22, which is **4**: finding fulfillment in smaller or more personal achievements.

Karmic Lessons

The numbers that are missing from our name represent the weak areas in our character, the lessons we are here to learn. For example, no 1s in a name would show there is a lack of self-confidence. Likewise, having many of the same number shows strength in that area. If there are five or more 1s, the person will have very strong opinions and, if spiritually immature, could very well be a bully.

All of us seem to have the same problems confronting us time after time. Chances are, they relate to the missing numbers, and when we know what they are they can be resolved.

For parents this is a major boon, for they will be able to help the child strengthen these potential weaknesses early in life. Then they will be better equipped to handle problems later on.

If you have a missing number and you cannot see where it applies to you, check the major numbers on your chart. It may be strong there. Suppose you have a missing 3. There may be a 3 for the total of your vowels, consonants, total name, or birth date.

If it is the total of the vowels (Soul's Urge) it is not karmic, but it is a weak link and oftentimes something you desire. If it is the total of your consonants (Personality) or your Total Expression, it is part of your make-up. If it is your birth day, it is you at maturity; the Birth Path reveals it to be what you are here to do and will just have to work a little harder.

Some other areas where this number may be found are:

Physical: You express these qualities in your work or in a physical manner.

Mental: This is used in your mental process and reasoning.

Emotional: Here it is expressed emotionally in both negative and positive aspects.

Intuitive: It is an *inner knowing* that needs to be brought into awareness.

Challenge: This reveals the time frame when you will have need of these qualities through circumstance.

Opportunity: This reveals the time frame when this lesson will be learned and used for success. It will be difficult to achieve goals until this happens.

Inner Guidance: Your higher self is gently prodding you to use the positive side of this number, knowing it will solve problems for you.

Golden Goal: If this is the only place it shows up, you will be faced with this lesson later in life. It will dawn on you that this is something that has been missing in your life.

Following are the Karmic Lessons for each vibration. Keep in mind that these lessons are something new to learn for growth and understanding.

KARMIC LESSON MINUS-1

Weakness

More interested in others than self. Lacks determination and confidence. Often very shy. Too dependent on others. Dreads starting something new. Must learn to stand up for self and make own decisions.

Remedy

Make a list of all your strong points to help you realize your worth. Next, list your weaknesses. Choose a weakness to make it a strength. For example, if you are really shy, take a course in speaking. Once you stand up before a group of people, you have put energy into that area and it becomes easier. Train yourself to stand up for yourself. Refuse to be persuaded or pressured by others. Become assertive, independent. If you have depended on other people to make decisions for you, you need to learn to trust your inner guidance. The chapter on your Inner Guidance Number should help you.

Child

Minus-1 children need to develop self-confidence. Let them make simple decisions to start with: "Here is a blue shirt and a yellow one. Which do you want to wear today?" Always praise them for jobs well done. To excel in a sport, musical instrument, or any creative activity will do wonders. They must be taught to be self-reliant at an early age, or the parents may find the child all grown and still depending on them.

KARMIC LESSON MINUS-2

Weakness

Uncooperative. No consideration for others and uncaring concerning their sensitivities. They will be forced to learn how to cooperate. Impatient with people. Bluntness may hurt people's feelings. May have difficulty in relating to women, or, if a woman, the masculine traits are stronger than the feminine: more aggressive than receptive. Feels clumsy with hands. Not too dexterous, so it may be difficult to handle work with small objects.

Remedy

It is necessary to learn to be tactful and diplomatic when dealing with people. Once we show concern for their feelings we receive from them, in return, a positive response. Once we thrill to that kind of response, it is easier for us to be more cooperative. The truth is, we automatically react to other people. If they are having an attitude problem we seem to automatically give that same attitude back to them. Practice doing otherwise and see what a difference it makes. Return a smile and a gentle word for a frown. Make a game of it for a while, and you'll see that you can be the actor and let them react to you. Once you feel the thrill for having received a positive response, the easier it will be to keep a cheerful attitude, which, in turn, helps you to be more cooperative. Pay more attention to details. As much as you may hate it, read the fine print on contracts. Purchase a magnifying glass to make it simpler. It could save you money.

Child

Minus-2 children need to learn how to play nicely with other children. They think of everything as their own, so teach them how to share. Have games that two or more can play constructively together.

Often this child will break things for lack of manual dexterity. Learning to play the piano or other musical instrument is a worthwhile investment. And they need soft, beautiful music in their lives. Loud, raucous music is antagonistic to their development.

KARMIC LESSON MINUS-3

Weakness

Self-expression is very difficult because of a lack of confidence, or feelings of inferiority. For some, the confidence is there but it is difficult to put their thoughts into words. They aren't very romantic due to shyness and feeling unable to express themselves well. They feel they must be apologetic and that comes across as a weakness.

Remedy

There is a strong need here to take on a happier attitude; lighten up. It seems that lack of confidence and an unhappy countenance go hand in hand. Never be overly apologetic. Just stand up straight and look people right in the eye. In fact, be sure to always stand up straight. The lack of self-esteem shows outwardly by a person's posture. A stooped shouldered stance shows you are trying to make yourself invisible so you won't be noticed. Confidence grows with knowledge. Find a subject you really like and learn all you can about it. To be expert in one thing does more for confidence than learning a little about a lot of things, but that doesn't hurt, either. Develop some creative talents. If you feel a lack of verbal ability it would be helpful to enroll in a speech class or the Dale Carnegie speaking program, join a toastmasters' club, or take part in a play.

Child

Minus-3 children need a lot of love, and praise and to know they are worthwhile. Developing talents is very important to building self-esteem. Read happy and informative stories to them and encourage the reading habit. Dancing and music lessons are wonderful plusses, and fun too. Just don't let them waste time by fooling around. It is important for them to have a good education.

KARMIC LESSON MINUS-4

Weakness

Hates work unless it is fun. Unorganized. Lacks concentration, especially if disinterested. May be claustrophobic and just can't work well in small places. Neither reliable nor practical. Sometimes they haven't needed to work so hard because others give so much help. Or perhaps they would prefer having someone else do the work. They may fear that work will be difficult and limiting and will look for an easy way out. Life can be very hard on those whose good work patterns are not developed.

Remedy

The lack of 4 is overcome by finding the work you love and, if that's not possible at the time, finding an appreciation for the work of the moment for the purpose it serves. It will help to develop organizational skills. Don't rush. Pay attention to details and work slowly and carefully. This is a must for minus-4.

Child

Minus-4 children must learn at an early age to keep their own room neat and have specific chores to do. By showing them step-by-step the best way to do things, they will never forget. Start them early in writing thank-you notes, too, and expressing their appreciation verbally.

KARMIC LESSON MINUS-5

Weakness

Five is the vibration of freedom and it is interesting to note that most Americans have at least one 5 in the name, whereas in very poor countries under dictatorship there are none. However, when the 5 is missing there is too much fear of new experiences and a lack of adaptability. Impending change can disrupt the person's whole life, and as a result their growth is restricted, causing a loss of opportunities. The Minus-5 hates to be in crowds, and that is not really so bad except there are times when it is unavoidable.

Remedy

Become more adaptable and you will be more relaxed. But do face your challenges fearlessly and confidently when you know you are right. It will help to read books such as Dale Carnegie's *How to Win Friends and Influence People* and Norman Vincent Peale's *The Power of Positive Thinking* and to use these principles to master your problems and enhance relationships.

Child

Minus-5 children need variety to help them adapt to change and lose fear of it. Short trips to interesting places such as the zoo and a day at the local roller/ice skating rink are helpful. Allow and encourage these children to make their own choices, and praise all their first worthwhile efforts.

KARMIC LESSON MINUS-6

Weakness

The Minus-6 does not have a strong sense of duty. Fears commitments and hates to take on responsibility. Domestic difficulties are not taken seriously. Unattractive voice quality or occasional voice problems. Will start projects and leave things undone. Does not have a talent for drawing or have an artistic sense.

Remedy

If domestic chores have been ignored, choose one at a time to conquer. For example, purchase a good basic cookbook, such as Betty Crocker's, and learn to cook one meal well by following the recipe step-by-step. Take pride in decorating one room and keeping it spotless. Take some cookies to some children or seniors in a local hospital. Show them you care. Then allow yourself to bask in the feeling of deep appreciation you get in return from them. Make a point to finish what you start. If yours is a voice with an unattractive quality, take singing lessons or work on it alone with a tape recorder, trying various tone expressions. Keep practicing the best sound until it comes naturally. The lack of 6 can be overcome by developing an appreciation for beauty and working to achieve it. Beautify your surroundings to give you a sense of peaceful satisfaction. Consciously think happy thoughts and they will be reflected on your face. ·

Child

Minus-6 children must be taught to appreciate their home and see the value in responsibilities. Small children can be taught to clean up their own messes and to put away their toys, even do their own laundry when shown how, especially if it is made to look like fun. They should be taught the joy found in helping others. It is often wise for these children to care for a pet. Show the beauty of color combinations in nature and have coloring books and art projects available for spare time.

KARMIC LESSON MINUS-7

Weakness

Either fearful or completely lacking caution. Never suspects hidden motives. Spiritual life may be neglected or restricted by dogma, which is nothing more than man's opinions on what truth ought to be. Because people with the missing 7 are not analytical or cautious, they are more open-minded than most people, so there is more inner happiness. But there is often a need for caution as a protective measure. They rarely take time away from work to relax.

Remedy

The 7 is strong because it gathers a lot of knowledge from reading and other methods, so the remedy is simple: Read more. Study philosophy and search for truth because truth eliminates fear. But keep that open mind. There is a need to find a balance between work and play. Find an enjoyable recreation. Most 7s would prefer an opera to a ball game, but whichever is preferred do take time to either enjoy a performance or take part in one. There is definitely a need to question and be cautious about certain things.

Child

Minus-7 children should be encouraged to read good things that will expand the mind in a positive and loving way. They need to know that there is a *loving* God. These children are so very trusting they must be taught to be cautious and not to try anything without knowing the consequences. It never occurs to them that there could be anyone or anything out there that could hurt them. When the child is older, find out what science is most appealing and encourage study of it by gifting the child with books on the subject. Or if you have a computer, there is software that will teach and delight a child in any of the sciences.

KARMIC LESSON MINUS-8

Weakness

The missing 8 can indicate a nasty temper, a lack of money or the propensity to spend carelessly. It can mean a weak body and/or ill health. If yours is a terrible temper, it will make you unattractive and be detrimental to you in work and relationships.

Remedy

From now on, when you feel yourself losing your temper, take mental note of the cause. Write it down so you don't forget. At another time, when you're in a better frame of mind, read it over and ask yourself, "Was this worth making me look stupid? What was the result of the emotional outburst, other than degrading myself? How could I have handled this better?" Think of someone whom you admire who has control. How would that person have handled the emotion? Decide right now to practice self-control and an alternative method for reaction and stick with it. Remember: Our choice of words is important, for they are the servants of our ideas and also reveal our character.

If the health is not up to par it may be from emotional reactions, wrong eating habits, and/or lack of exercise. Decide that you will, for one week, eliminate fast foods, fried foods, soda pop, and beer. Drink a glass or 8-oz. bottle of fresh spring water first thing in the morning and often during the day. Eat mainly fresh fruits and vegetables. Then plan to do it a second week. Fruits are cleansers; vegetables are builders. Fruits digest quickly and go right into the bloodstream, so they should be eaten first. Once you get use to this diet, you won't want to go back to sugary drinks and "junk food." Don't deprive yourself of a luscious piece of dessert once in a while. Enjoy it. If you hate to exercise, take brisk walks.

Child

Minus-8 children should definitely be given an allowance, taught to save a portion and to spend the remainder wisely, or there could well be financial problems in later life. They may have a temper, so they must learn self-control early and be praised for it. Don't allow them to eat junk foods as a main diet. Encourage health-conscious habits.

KARMIC LESSON MINUS-9

Weakness

If there are no 9s on any of the major areas of your chart, as well as missing from your Birth Name, there may well be a lack of tolerance or concern for others and a tendency to be very critical. Minus-9s spend too much time judging others while being oblivious to their own shortcomings. They may be kind and helpful but will lack the good feeling that should accompany acts of kindness.

Remedy

There is a need to understand other people. Without understanding, we become critical and judge them harshly. There is an old Indian saying that one must walk miles in another's shoes before criticizing them. It will be helpful to study the world's religions in order to understand their beliefs, because a person's religion often dictates the way they live and respond. A helpful guide to understanding people is Dale Carnegie's *How to Make Friends and Influence People.* There are other helpful books on psychology that will increase one's respect and tolerance for people in general. Even better is to do something kind for someone. The warm glow you feel is such a treasure. I have met some people I found difficult to like at first. If I knew I had to work with them or see them for some reason, I would talk with them and find something of interest we had in common. I would keep that positive link in mind each time, and I found that by focusing on a positive quality we could have an amicable relationship. The secret is in the point of your focus.

Child

Minus-9 children should be taught the joy of giving and to be considerate of the feelings of other people—or you could have a bully on your hands. A firm but loving hand is important, for these children need to feel loved and will learn loving ways by example, for the 9 influence makes them very impressionable. Never allow them to see violent movies for this reason. It is important to have a firm foundation of compassion and brotherly love.

KARMIC LESSON MINUS-0

(No missing numbers.)

When there are no missing numbers there is an awareness of all of the lessons. This does not mean there won't be any difficulties or problems, but the understanding will be greater in handling them.

The Planes of Expression

Part A: Numbers on the Planes of Expression

1 ON THE PLANES OF EXPRESSION

Average (1–3)	Many	None
Will power. Charm.	Strong opinions.	Not self-centered.
Confident. Witty.	Strong interests.	
Determination.	Courageous.	
Individuality.	Leadership.	
	Articulate. Willful.	

Negative: Pushy. Self centered. No initiative. Ego dominates. No confidence. Offensive. Wants to control others. A pushover. Agitator. Gang leader.

1 on the Physical

Starts things easily with enthusiasm but hates to finish; would rather go on to next project. Friendly. A leader. Energetic. Fresh approach. Great endurance. Independent.

10

Prominent in some way. May become famous.

1 on the Mental

Much charm. Often ready with a witty comeback. Good ideas come easily. Will tackle personal goals with gusto. Very good in directing others, but does not like to be told what to do. Negative 1s are agitators.

1 on the Emotional

Strong-willed. Definite likes and dislikes. Changeable. Enthusiastic. Charming. Outgoing and sociable. Negative 1s get bored easily, are jumpy, and are sometimes uptight. Resentful. Takes things personally. No self-control. Demanding in relationships.

1 on the Intuitive

Relates self to all concepts. Has creative ideas. Gets hunches. Analyzes facts. Sensitive and imaginative.

Note: A 10 on any plane makes that person more dominant and powerful.

2 ON THE PLANES OF EXPRESSION

Average (1)	Many	None
Courteous. Helpful.	Appreciation of the	Uncooperative.
Cooperative. Shy.	arts and beauty.	Insensitive.
Very sensitive.	Diplomatic.	Urge to steal.
Friendly. Loves music.	Charming.	Not adaptable.
Emotional.		Inconsiderate.

Negative: Afraid of people. Easily hurt. Feelings of inferiority. Vibration of a liar.

2 on the Physical

Capable of fine, detailed work. Artistic. Can work easily with small objects. Musical talent. Likes to collect things. Sensitive and caring. May worry too much. Happiest in harmonious, peaceful surroundings. Negative 2s are idle, lazy, careless, and unreliable.

11

A healer; has gift for spiritual healing. A negative 11 can reach total depravity and suffering.

2 on the Mental

Sees both sides of the question and is more tolerant and understanding than most people. Is naturally cooperative, so makes a fine companion. Good at accumulating facts that, in turn, can make for strong opinions. Needs peace. Negative 2s are connivers and schemers; crooked in deals. Liars.

2 on the Emotional

Very emotional. Music moves them deeply. Desires a beautiful environment with everything just so. Needs to be loved and understood. Aloneness depresses them so they seek companionship. Feels deeply for others' hurts. Negative 2s can be overly sensitive; cry easily, be too fastidious, picky.

2 on the Intuitive

Feels good will towards all people and finds it hard to understand why no one else does. Has some spiritual awareness. They are easily influenced. They should not fool with the occult because of a psychic response. They simply cannot understand why there have to be wars; why people cannot settle their differences in a mature and sensible way without killing each other. The negative 2 can be fanatic, rebellious. They don't always trust in their own decisions.

3 ON THE PLANES OF EXPRESSION

Average (1 or 2)	Many	None
Social, but not personality plus. Lacks confidence. Careless. Lazy. Scatters energies.	Good with words. Many talents. Very expressive. Extravagant. Good imagination.	Difficulty with verbal expression. No confidence, for lack of communication skills. Not romantic. Lacks concentration.

Negative: Wants all fun, no work. Overly talkative. Gossips. Self-centered. Hates to have to think hard.

3 on the Physical

Creative with hands artistically and/or musically. Not too organized, for 3 is more creative than practical. Hates to face facts. Will use imagination to get things done. Most 3s are attractive. They have a childlike quality. Loves pleasure, hates hard work, and will try to make work fun. Wants companionship.

3 on the Mental

Wonderful creative ideas come easily. Has much imagination. Is usually very interesting to listen to. Does not take life too seriously. They express themselves easily; never at a loss for words. On the negative side, they talk too much. Careless about order. Fail to plan. Boastful. Lack concentration. A bluffer.

3 on the Emotional

Easy-going, happy, optimistic, and fun to be around. Wants to be well-liked. Needs a creative outlet. Loves to uplift others and bring joy into their lives. Often acts on impulse. On the negative side, they talk too much or gossip.

3 on the Intuitive

Finds beauty in expressing highest values and can inspire others. Has a natural psychic tendency. Does not need a script; speech flows from creative thought, so they are good at improvisation. Negative 3s gossip or become silent and unsociable; will not communicate. Inferiority complex.

4 ON THE PLANES OF EXPRESSION

Average (1)	Many	None
Warm-hearted.	Great concentration.	Unorganized
Concentration.	Good planners. Builders.	Claustrophobic.
Gets things done.	Needs to keep busy.	Lazy (if no 2s, 6s,
	Disciplined.	or 8s).

Negative: Stubborn. Argumentative. Dull. Too serious. Is right at all costs. Feels limited. Narrow-minded. Resents authority. Hates change. Explosive temper.

4 on the Physical

Hard worker. Wants to work slowly and do well. Likes routine. Has stick-to-itiveness. Will easily accomplish work ideas given by others. Practical and dependable. Organizer. Loves family. Determined to win over opposition. Very good with hands: mechanical, painting, mending, musically, or in sports. Warm-hearted and generous. The negative 4 is stubborn and argumentative. Is right at all costs. Quick temper.

4 on the Mental

A planner who gets things done. Serious-minded. Honest and straightforward. Will stand behind his word. Good manager or boss. Organized. Prefers being in business for self or being the authority. Rarely gets bored for mind is always occupied with something. Very strong opinions. Does not like to be rushed.

Determined to follow through once the mind is set. Has a practical approach to problems. The negative 4 can be tied down with family problems.

4 on the Emotional

Does not like to show emotion; holds it back. Is patient. Family is important and shown generosity and love. Dislikes being subordinate. Can be bullheaded and will argue. Wants order. Resentful of authority. Possessive; will fight for what he believes is his (persons or things). Needs to have work appreciated. The negative 4 has an explosive temper. Can't stand being told what to do.

4 on the Intuitive

Believes in things seen. Does not care for the abstract. May argue religion. Analytical. Either prefers religion with ritual and display or one that will give practical answers for everyday living. Takes a practical approach to religion. Can do practical things with ideas. Negative 4s have closed minds when it comes to discussion.

5 ON THE PLANES OF EXPRESSION

Average (3–5)	Many	None
Intelligent.	Loves people,	Not aggressive.
Versatile.	travel, and change.	Hates crowds.

Wants fun.	Versatile. Adaptable.	Wants to be left
Friendly.	Curious.	alone.
Sociable.	Loves freedom.	Not adaptable.
	Looks forward to	Nervousness.
	vacation.	Feels limited.
	Good talkers,	
	salespeople.	
	Friendly, outgoing,	
	and sociable.	

Negative: Critical of others. Impatient. Impulsive. Temper. Nervousness. Over-sure. Possessive. Strong sex appetite. Takes chances. Apt to act before thinking. 2nd vibration of the Liar (2, 5, 9).

5 on the Physical

Loves to travel and be with people. Gets bored easily and becomes restless if there is no variety. Here we find the daring ones: stuntmen, stuntwomen, racers, and gamblers. Also excellent salesmen and mechanics. They know what makes products sell or motors run. Promoters. Hates routine. Must be free to come and go and to move about. No office work for them! Progressive nature. Observant. Loves excitement. Doers, not watchers.

5 on the Mental

Curious about everything and will seek out answers. Good at researching. May have several things going at once. Very intelligent, inquiring nature. May be over-sure of self. Will try new things. Adapts to change. Quite critical of others.

5 on the Emotional

Restless. Wants to know why others feel as they do. Needs variety and so adapts easily to new surroundings. They value their freedom. They want to be popular. Negative 5s are not very patient and may be critical of others, nervous, and have a temper. They may drink too much or overeat when frustrated.

5 on the Intuitive

Quite intuitive, but doesn't always realize it. Can grasp an idea and explain it well. Quick to catch on. Will not accept religion at face value and will look for answers everywhere when interested. A "live and let live" attitude. They are receptive to ideas, good or bad.

6 ON THE PLANES OF EXPRESSION

Average (3–5)	Many	None
Responsible.	Strong sense	Hates heavy
Humanitarian.	of responsibility.	responsibilities.
Artistic.	Wants to serve.	Not aware of
Idealist.	Artistic ability.	duties.
Good teachers,	Very strong/	Often lucky.
counselors,	set opinions.	Takes problems
doctors, nurses.	Very domestic.	lightly.

Negative: Strict. Dominant. Demanding. Holier than thou. Insists others live up to its demands and accept its opinions. Demands loyalty. Over-sexed. Physically abusive. Domestic tyranny.

6 on the Physical

Doesn't mind responsibility. Will help others. Likes surroundings to be attractive and comfortable. Artistic nature. A natural teacher. Good with children. Physically strong; capable of handling the sick, aged, and disabled. Loves to bring comfort to those who need it. A natural nurturer. Loves a garden to work in and enjoy. Natural singing voice. Needs love and affection. Negative 6s think of nothing but sex and can be physically abusive.

6 on the Mental

Tends to worry about little things. Feels responsible and will attend to duties. Make fine teachers, for they have the gift of words for putting over ideas. Make good parents, and good community leaders. Cares for humanity, if not negative. Can feel burdened. Negative 6s are smug, self-righteous; want to pass laws to make people conform to their values.

6 on the Emotional

Wants to do the right thing and is most appreciative when praised. Loves beauty around. Has a good sense of color. Appreciates art, music, and the finer things of life. Ideals are so high; few can live up to their expectations. Negative 6s must be careful not to be preachy and dominant; are hard on family; yet they resent a demanding attitude. Wants proper discipline and can overdo it. Demands loyalty. Wants love and approval at all times. Worries when not shown appreciation.

6 on the Intuitive

Artistic. They intuitively know what is right. Can be fine counselors, advisors, or ministers. Expect everyone to have as high ideals as they and are disappointed when they do not. They sometimes have trouble putting their ideas to work, for it is easier to see things accomplished in mind than it is to actually do them.

7 ON THE PLANES OF EXPRESSION

Average (0–1)	Many	None
Discriminating.	Unusual viewpoint.	Not cautious.
Wants to know why.	Loves research.	More open-minded.
Likes to prove things.	Technical abilities.	Accepts surface
Analytical. Scientific.	Mathematic.	appearances.
Specialized skills.	Thinker. Very clever.	Lack of spiritual
Loves to read.	Strong opinions	awareness.
	on politics and	
	religion.	

Negative: If uneducated, turns to schemes, hidden motives. Secretive. Drinking. Repression. Sex complexes. Weird behavior. Not a good mixer. Dislikes people.

7 on the Physical

Aloof. Dignified. Reserved, even mysterious. Stands out in the crowd with eyes full of wisdom. Excellent in any scientific field because of powers of analysis. Seems standoffish; friendly with a select few. Should not work with the public; prefers to work alone or with intellectual equals. Not a physical laborer. Literary.

7 on the Mental

Perfectionist who likes to work alone. Introverted. Clever. Has mathematical skills. Delves into things. Happy in own thought world.

Enjoys conversing mainly with those they feel comfortable with, or those they impart knowledge to—or can learn from. Can keep secrets. These are thinkers who solve problems through intuition. Negative 7s have very strange, perverted ideas.

7 on the Emotional

Has good self control, but tends to hold much inside. Can become frustrated for lack of an outlet. Finds many creative concepts through meditation or deep thought. Appreciates the finer things. Wants so much, sometimes to the point of frustration. Want to be surrounded by beauty. Likes nature, especially plants. Hates to be hemmed in, such as with apartment living. Charming, warm, and humorous with friends; cold, distant, and uncomfortable around strangers. Hates to show emotions. The negative 7 is either silent or sarcastic.

7 on the Intuitive

Highly intuitive. Studies and understands deep concepts and is able to teach them to others. Here we often find writers, composers, and highly creative people. Takes to psychic, philosophical, esoteric, and/or theosophical concepts. The negative 7 closes the mind to anything esoteric. Feels bitter.

8 ON THE PLANES OF EXPRESSION

Average (1)	Many	None
Can work under pressure.	Very efficient.	Careless with money.
Fine character.	Attracts money and is money-conscious.	Does not care about material values.
Good judgment.	Innate business sense.	
Can meet difficult situations.	Commands respect.	
	Can implement ideas.	Needs a manager.

Negative: Very material-minded. Needs the best of everything to prove self-worth. Overly money-conscious. Stress on personal achievement. An overachiever. Appears forceful and dominant. Great self-importance. Wants status and power. Frustrated when they cannot achieve more. Lives an intense life with many problems.

8 on the Physical

A go-getter. Ambitious to handle things on a large scale with authority and power. A born leader. Great physical endurance; if not business-minded, might be drawn to sports or to music, or dance. Always active. Enjoys being on the go either mentally or physically. Wants material satisfaction. Bounces back from illness quickly; is seldom sick. Negative 8s use their brute strength to get their way by force.

8 on the Mental

Wants power and position and is ambitious to achieve it. Works hard for money. Very good in business and wants the recognition of a job well done. Excellent judgment and organizational abilities and knows it.

Negative 8s are too bossy and domineering. Conceited. There may be many tests and trials to go through.

8 on the Emotional

Needs to look prosperous to others as a matter of self-pride. Feels best dressed-up looking at their best. Strong emotional nature. Moved by music. Parents deal firmly with children, and believe in discipline. Will marry for money for sake of image or business opportunity. On the negative side, never satisfied.

8 on the Intuitive

Can put intuitive ideas into practical use. Businesslike even in spiritual matters. Can organize and direct spiritual/religious ventures.

9 ON THE PLANES OF EXPRESSION

Average (3)	Many	None
Compassionate.	Loved by all.	No compassion.
Tolerant.	Generous.	Not aware of
Good will.	Very creative.	others' feelings.
Understanding.	Great imagination.	May be helpful
	Literary.	and kind, but
	Impressionable.	without emotion.
	Thoughtful.	Dramatic.
	Grateful.	Forgiving.

Negative: Over-emotional. Overly sensitive. Moody. Too impressionable. Habits are easily started and hard to break. May overeat or drink when unhappy. Needs approval. Hard to reason with. The 3rd vibration of the liar (2, 5, 9).

9 on the Physical

Nines are impressionable and very dramatic. They make good publishers, importers, and exporters. Those who are especially good in the limelight: actors, writers, instructors, and orators. As performers, they need someone to direct them. They are the actors, not the directors. They are not physical laborers, nor are they mental giants. They act on intuition and impressions. Strong viewpoints. Romantics. Great lovers. Disappointments hit them pretty hard. It is best they do not drink, or they really overdo it.

9 on the Mental

Can work easily with all kinds of people, for they are tolerant and compassionate. They need to know the value of attending to priorities. They tend to forget immediate concerns while daydreaming about their big plans, but they do not forget family birthdays or anniversaries. They hate details.

9 on the Emotional

Very creative and very dramatic. They do everything with style. They love admiration from fans, have great pride and feeling of self-importance. Artistic nature. Add dramatic flair to all they do and in what they wear. They enjoy crowds, especially if they can entertain them and receive their enthusiastic response. They need love and are very romantic. Negative 9s must be careful not to start bad habits for they are hard for them to break. They have big egos. Can appear cold.

9 on the Intuitive

Has wonderful dreams but does not always carry them through. Is capable of inspiring others. Not at all practical and easily swayed. Needs love. Is romantic and an idealist.

Note: Nines are impressionable on all planes.

0 ON THE PLANES OF EXPRESSION

(The missing number on the planes.)

A cipher (0) does not necessarily mean a fault. Knowing the weakness that may be pointed out by the cipher is like having a key to unlock a mystery. It signifies a plane where the person needs work through study and application. When this missing attribute is worked on, the problems that have plagued that person will start to disappear.

0 on the Physical

(No 4s or 5s in the name.)

Not much stamina. Does not apply self due to lack of energy.

0 on the Mental

(No 1s or 8s in the name.)

Even with no mental letters, the person can be very intelligent. Very difficult to make decisions. Needs to develop willpower. Not a logical thinker. If there are more numbers on the emotional level, will respond emotionally rather than intellectually.

0 on the Emotional

(No 2s, 3s or 6s in the name.)

Hard to express emotions, so appears cold. May have very little feeling for others.

0 on the Intuitive

(No 7s or 9s in the name.)

Not at all interested in abstract ideas. Does not believe in intuition. Unforgiving.

Note: Most likely those numbers will be quite strong elsewhere in the chart. Sometimes any more of them could well be an over-intensification of that numerical vibration.

Part B: Letters on the Planes of Expression

Before going further, it may be helpful to view these two charts. In Chart 5 you can see at a glance the letter groupings and their Plane of Expression. Chart 6 gives you an easy clue for each root number to make it easier for you to remember them.

Note: The Planes of Expression are Physical, Mental, Emotional, and Intuitive levels of consciousness, and we will take them in that order. This means we will not start this section with number 1, which is a mental vibration, but with 4, which is physical. By number, the planes are:

Physical - **4, 5** Mental - **1, 8** Emotional -**2, 3, 6** Intuitive - **7, 9.**

Chart 5:
Full and Root Numbers of Letters

Full Numbers			Root Numbers		Plane
1 -A	10 -J	19 -S	=1	A J S	Mental
2-B	11-K	20-T	=2	B K T	Emotional
3-C	12-L	21-U	=3	C L U	Emotional
4-D	13-M	22-V	=4	D M V	Physical
5-E	14-N	23-W	=5	E N W	Physical
6-F	15-O	24-X	=6	F O X	Emotional
7-G	16-P	25-Y	=7	G P Y	Intuitive
8-H	17-Q	26-Z	=8	H Q Z	Mental
9-I	18-R		=9	I R	Intuitive

Chart 6:
Easy Reference to Letter/Number Traits

1-10-19	An easy way to remember the 1 Letters is to think of A J S as Ages. Every age has a beginning, and 1 marks that beginning. All 1s have creative ideas and start them going.
2-11-20	An easy way to remember the 2 Letters is to think of B K T as bucket. All 2s are sensitive, with enough emotions to fill a bucket!
3-12-21	An easy way to remember the 3 Letters is to think of C L U as "a clue," and the geometry of each letter gives a clue – or evidence of the character. Note that the 3 and its letters, the C, L, and U, are all open rather than closed in, signifying communication skills and "open to talk."
4-13-22	An easy way to remember the 4 letters is to think of D M V as the Department of Motor Vehicles. All motor vehicles with the exception of big rigs have four tires. Plus, that agency issues the driver's license that people must have in order to drive to work. The 4 is a vibration of working to manifest money for a secure future.
5-14-23	An easy way to remember the 5 letters is to think of E N W as an anagram for NEW. The 5 vibration is constantly seeking new adventures and knowledge. They love their freedom and want to try, test, and taste what life has to offer.
6-15-24	An easy way to remember the 6 letters is to think of F O X as being the clever and sly animal, for their root is 6, or 666 (which many people fear). The 6 has to do with the three-dimensional physical plane where everything that exists has 6 sides: North, South, East, West, Up, and Down.
7-16-25	An easy way to remember the 7 letters, G P Y, is to think of them as a gyp. It seems to people on the spiritual path that they must be gypped of a prosperous physical life when their interests are spiritual in nature.
8-17-26	An easy way to think of the 8 letters, H Q Z, is as "each quiz," for 8 is the number of the executive, and in order to get to that point they have had to pass each quiz.
9-18	The easy way to remember the 9 letters, I and R, is to think of them as saying, "I are." This is another way of saying, "I Am," which implies completeness.

THE PHYSICAL LETTERS FOR **4: D M V**

All 4s are hard workers. Economical and practical. Organizers. Good at details. They do not mind routine work. They work well with their hands, creatively, musically, or mechanically. Like to work slowly, patiently, at own pace.

D (4)

Positive

Reliable. Efficient. Strong. Loves nature. Loyal. Honest. Good at completing things. Adores their family and country.

Negative

Indecisive. Opinionated. Argumentative. Too independent for own good. Too straight-laced. Stubborn. Feels closed in.

M (13)

Positive

Excellent memory. Gives good advice and likes to give good service. Good to children and their own people. Good manager. Has business capabilities. Works well in small spaces. Artistically creative (due to the 1 and 3). Loves deeply but does not often show it.

Negative

Often feels hemmed in. Hard and unfeeling. Believes only in things seen; wants proof! Temperamental. Careless. Accident-prone. Colds and headaches. Hidden emotional problems. Cannot relax.

V (22)

Positive

Open and receptive to ideas and can make them work. Very intellectual. Understands business. Very capable leaders. Not idle talkers. They simply have to help people.

Negative

Suspicious. Selfish. They magnify their difficulties. Strong mind, but often a weak body. Nervous breakdowns if confined. Takes risky chances. Misused sexual energy.

THE PHYSICAL LETTERS FOR 5: E N W

The 5s need more diversion than 4s because of many interests. They must have freedom in order to accomplish. Impulsive. Not as patient as 4.

E (5)

Positive

Helpful. Practical. Daring. E is a symbol for *energy*, both physical and spiritual. Desires knowledge. Has interest in all occult teachings. Mystical, psychic, and romantic. Gets experience in many things. Manual dexterity. Good at making and fixing things.

Negative

Restless. Has to be doing something. Too sensual; self-indulgence could lead to poor health. Deceitful. Liar. Irresponsible.

N (14)

Positive

Loves people, travel, and change. Ambitious desire for material things. Likes peppy music and dancing. A clear thinker. Wins arguments with reason and logic. Imaginative. Emotional.

Negative

Restless; always wants to be doing something. Daring. Takes risky chances. Selfish. Stubborn. Argumentative.

W(23)

Positive

A good letter for business. Will get things done. Needs to work where there is a lot of activity. A well-developed mind. Invents ideas. Good eye for colors. Loves deeply. Very generous to those they love. As a vowel, seeks spirituality.

Negative

As a consonant, a strong force that gives great power to good people; to lesser souls, it will be unstable and very limiting. Overlyconfident. Impatient. Acts too fast and then regrets it. Either carefree with money or miserly. Ill of health.

THE MENTAL LETTERS FOR 1: A J S

Many religious leaders had names with the initial J: Jesus, John the Baptist, James and John the Apostles; Jacob, who became the father of the Jewish nation; Jeremiah, a major prophet of the Old Testament; and Joshua, Son of Nun, who took Moses' place.

All 1s have strong will. Determination. Initiative. Ambition. Leadership. Individuality. Use imagination along with facts. Likes to do things in own way.

A (1)

Positive

Inspired. Likes to starts things, not finish. Active and ambitious. Creative. Confident. Original.

Negative

Jealous. Dictatorial. Big ego. Blunt. Self-important. Materialistic.

J (10)

Positive

Inspired. Humorous. Witty. Good memory. Leadership ability. Not a natural follower. Wants an advanced position. Cautious and clever. Often religious.

Negative

Same as A, but more power to overcome weakness. Dishonest. Vacillates. Does not always finish what it starts.

S (19)

Positive

A letter of wisdom. Spiritual. Quick in thought and action. Many interests. Emotional and caring. Achieves through own efforts. Must be alone to accomplish anything.

Negative

Self-centered. Relates everything to self because $1+9 = 10$; $1+0= 1$. Depressed. Cannot take orders. All negative qualities of 1 and 10.

THE MENTAL LETTERS FOR 8: H Q Z

All 8s can work under pressure. Mind power. Good judgment. Logical deduction. A need for personal achievement.

H (8)

Positive

Good concentration. Mind power. Endurance. Independence. Alert. Aware. Watchful. Planner. Organizer. Logical. Good reasoning abilities. Lovable leader.

Negative

Terrible tyrant. Demanding. Intolerant. Suspicious. Revengeful. Uses poison words. Foul-mouthed and vulgar. Fearful. Slow. Dull. Mental strain. Selfish. Miser.

Q (17)

Positive

Honest. Genius potential. Many interests. Active mentally and physically. Desires to live the good life. Wants harmony and comfort in home. Wants a partner to be proud of. Is Charming and loyal. Good to be with. Dependable. Practical. Conservative. Sympathetic.

Negative

Peculiar personalities. Uncertain habits. Demanding of others. Greedy. Materialistic. Temporary insanity.

Z (26)

Positive

Analyzes everything. Gives power to a name and strengthens the other letters. Natural psychic gifts through intuition and inspiration. Cannot abuse power without negative results.

Negative

Mental breakdowns. Needs rest. May act strange. Easily influenced in wrong environment. Misdirected energies. Sly. Greedy. Deceptive. Exaggerates. Not comfortable in sharing. Not a good marriage partner.

THE EMOTIONAL LETTERS FOR 2: B K T

All 2s are dualities. All 2s are very sensitive, are easily hurt, and have a keen sense of touch. They need companionship, love to please, and are deeply moved by music.

B (2)

Positive

Fall in love easily. Make wonderful companions, considerate partners. Love, want, and need a home. Most are very neat. Moved deeply by good music; hate noise. Love to collect and appreciate nice things. Sociable. Loving.

Negative

Need a lot of self-control. Moody. Lazy. Untidy. Materialistic. Sneaky. Secretive. Quick to get hurt and easily offended. Lives too much in the emotions. Overly shy. Needs to be in love or cannot function.

K (11)

Positive

A high spiritual letter; brings light, laughter, and inspiration to all. An emotional intuitive who wants to master the lower self. Open and receptive. Inspired intuition. Simply must help others, so needs an understanding partner.

Negative

Too emotional. Nervous tension leads to breakdowns. Easily led. Dishonest. Glib. Deceptive. Dislikes detail, routine. Intolerant of others' sensitivities. Desire to collect things can result in thievery, kleptomania.

Note: Eleven is the hardest of all vibrations as it demands such high standards, it is hard for others to meet them. Incredible frustration results from standards and goals not attained. Ancients called 11 "the path of the penitent."

T (20)

Positive

T is more spiritual than B. Eager for enlightenment. Travel is important, as are music and collecting things. Orderly and neat. Helpful and charming. Will carry the load for you (note the strong shoulders of the T).

Negative

A testing letter, carries a cross. Concerned with self-sacrifice. Strains emotionally and physically. Cannot concentrate. Expects too much of people. Easily hurt. Too fussy about details; frustrated if others mess up. Difficulty making decisions because of seeing both points of view. Blunt. Stubborn. Picky.

Note: Double T (tt) means tied-up conditions when annoyed. Will double-cross self.

THE EMOTIONAL LETTERS FOR 3: C L U

All 3s are imaginative, creative, and good with words. They have a wonderful childlike quality.

C (3)

Positive

Expresses self freely and happily. Psychic, but usually unaware of it. It "sees" (Cs). C is designed as a half moon to symbolize its intuitive nature and strong emotions (The moon affects the tides and water is a symbol of emotion). Expressive, talkative, outgoing, and optimistic. Needs an artistic outlet.

Negative

Lacks self-expression. Becomes tongue-tied. Gossips. Either too self-satisfied or worries over every little thing. Poor loser. Too serious. Intolerant. Impulsive. Dissipates. Cannot handle money.

L (12)

Positive

Not as carefree and spontaneous as C. Happy disposition. Friendly. Sociable. Good voice. Loves singing. Good with words.

Negative

Too emotional. Inner sadness that is hard to explain. Fear. Sorrow. Frustration. Coldness.

U (21)

Positive

Executive ability. Intellectual. Determined. Excels in music. Good voice. Needs good education. Home life is important.

Negative

The least expressive of all 3s. Jealous. Nervous. Intense. Emotional. Sarcastic. Temperamental. Starts quarrels. Antagonistic.

THE EMOTIONAL LETTERS FOR 6: F O X

All 6s have strong emotions. Need appreciation. Desire to help others. Interest in own community. Strong opinions. Artistic flair. Good teachers, counselors.

F (6)

Positive

Fatherly, family-oriented. Loyal. Cares deeply. Artistic abilities. Loves music and harmony. Intuitive. Serves others. Loves to give. Always ready to help (see how F's arms reach out?). Responds to appreciation. Very responsible.

Negative

May feel burdened. Worries about others. Fussy. Meddlesome. Wants to control family. A know-it-all. Thinks everyone should believe as he or she does. Smug and self-righteous. Holier-than-thou. Uses voice as silent weapon. Domestic tyranny. Sexually demanding. Abusive.

O (15)

Positive

Symbol of the Sun; open and warm. Poised and secure. Conservative nature. All or nothing, as the circle suggests. Brings financial gain. Great imagination. Good writers. Home, children, love, and business are all important. A jack-of-all-trades; can do most anything. Very creative.

Negative

Destructive qualities. Impulsive. Sullen, sulky, and moody. Will not talk out their problems. Upset mentally. Worrisome. Jealous. Suspicious. Cynical. Tyrannical. Set opinions. Set ways. Possessive.

X (24)

Positive

Either spiritual or material, high-minded, or debased. Magnetic personality. Likes people and social life. Highly evolved Xs have intellectual strength and knowledge. They should be of public service. Music is important. Great desire to improve mankind.

Negative

The most karmic and difficult letter. Depicted as open and vulnerable on all sides. Constant state of turmoil. Takes advantage of people. Pleasure-seekers. Demands sexual gratification. Overindulges. Looks on the dark side of life. Revengeful. Irritable. Bad temper. No sympathy. Will X itself out.

THE INTUITIVE LETTERS FOR 7: G P Y

All 7s deal with technical facts. Analysis. Scientific and/or mathematical. Likes to uncover secrets. Interested in the occult and the unknown. Creative mind. Unusual viewpoints. Daydreamers.

G (7)

Positive

Likes to do things in a big way and determination to do it. Wise. Spiritual and psychic. Loves music. Relates to medicine; many doctors have this letter. Likes to work alone. Curious and investigative. Very selective. Generally does not like crowds and confusion.

Negative

Often difficult to understand, although they think otherwise. Shy. Stronger mentally than physically. Aloof. Deceptive. Morbid. Egoists. Critical of others and sarcastic. Use hateful words.

P (16)

Positive

Both physical and mental in nature. Intuitive. Self-sufficient. Versatile. Very talented. Has the ability to overcome obstacles. Needs study to attain a prominent position. A good education is vital if P is to be fulfilled.

Negative

Lacks the determination and willpower of G. Does not express innermost feelings. Argumentative. Aloof. Morbid. Moody. Deceptive. Ill-natured. Tactless. Intolerant. Domineering. A big head. Not a good marriage or business partner. Possessive. Must have sufficient rest.

Note: Although many are religious leaders, popes, parsons, priests, and pastors, others tend to be atheistic or agnostic.

Y (25)

Positive

Keen perceptive powers. Will speak only if there is something worth saying. Has a yearning to know deeper things (shaped like the dousing rod that seeks out water from a deeper level). Prefers silence and loves the beauty of nature. A daydreamer.

Negative

Desires to be free but seldom is. Can be the most beautiful or the most tragic. Restless. Sensitive. Depressed. Talkative. Truly negative Y turns to drink, sex, or drugs, ultimately harmful to themselves.

THE INTUITIVE LETTERS FOR 9: I R

The 9s possess an inner knowing. Abstract ideas. Very impressionable. Creative abilities. Humanitarian concerns. Understand and like people.

I (9)

Positive

This is a beautiful, high-powered vibration. Gentle. Artistic temperament. Magnetic. Intelligent. Active. Scientific. Capable of good friendships. Romantic. Needs music and the arts. Many creative abilities. Expresses self clearly and fluently. Good at starting things. Emotional and inspired, as well as intuitive.

Negative

Overactive. Touchy. Intolerant. Restless. Moody. Shiftless. Arrogant. Critical. Unsympathetic. Many who have this letter are destructive. Fanatical. Extremely self-centered.

R(18)

Positive

The most selfless and understanding letter of them all. Great tolerance. Gives personal and professional service. A dreamer of dreams. Psychic and intuitive. Good memory. Interested in literature and mysterious things. Likes to investigate strange events. Finds answers to other people's problems.

Negative

Gets into trouble with the law. Envious. Jealous. Bad temper. Rude. Rebellious. Rough. Self-seeking interests. Strong, physical desires.

Challenges and Opportunities

THE 9-YEAR CYCLES

There are four distinct periods of personal growth: childhood, youth, middle age, and the mature years. These four main cycles are the seasons of our life, the first being spring, a personal period of development; then summer, a time when we are either setting the foundation for our life's work or are already involved in it; autumn, during our middle age; and winter, just before and during our senior years.

Each period is governed by certain energies that color our feelings and affect our actions. These are very personal and relate to the development of our talents and attributes.

Our weaknesses and strengths coincide during these cycles. The weaknesses that need work are our *Challenges*. The energies themselves are called *Peaks, Pinnacles,* or *Opportunities*. These are 9-year cycles, the first and last having the longest duration. Nine years x 4 cycles =36. And because our birth date is individual to us for our personal cycles, we subtract our own Birth Path number from 36 to find the first cycle in our own life. This was discovered in the early 1930s by Dr. Walton of California and was tested and confirmed by the California Institute of Numerical Research.

In Chapter 2, you were shown how to find your Challenge and Opportunity numbers from your birth date. First we will discuss the Challenges.

131

Part A: Challenges

These numbers show us the areas in our life that need to be strengthened. They are warning signs that let us know that we must learn to use the positive aspects of those number vibrations during that cycle or we will have difficulties in handling problems. When we know these problem spots ahead of time, we can work on improving our actions and reactions until the weaknesses become our strengths. When that happens, the challenge is more easily met.

The very bottom number is your *Main Challenge,* which means it stays with you throughout your life, not just during the last cycle where it is most dominant.

To find your numbers, see Chapter 2. With your chart in front of you, compare your numbers with the details for each that follow.

THE 1 CHALLENGE: OVERCOME DEPENDENCE

The 1 is a personal challenge. During this time, people will try to sway you and it will be difficult for you because althought you want to please them, it doesn't necessarily please *you*, so you must develop your willpower. It is important to know that you can rely on your inner strength.

Don't ask people for their opinions. You won't learn this challenge until you stop leaning on others. Decide now to form your own conclusions, make your own decisions, and stand on your own. And be assertive about it. Respect your own individuality and realize that only you can be in charge of your life. You must be in control and still be considerate of others in the way that you deal with them.

Relatives or friends will try to push you to do things their way, or you have made some decisions that they don't like and they let you know it. You feel as though they are trying to control your life, and your resentment grows. The inner conflict can be enormous. First, you must set your resentment aside and take their point of view into consideration. They may be right and may save you from making a mistake that will come back to haunt you. Then again, they may be wrong. In that case, thank them for their concern and then handle the matter, as you feel best.

During this cycle, you will find that you have to do things yourself if they are to get done. Your will and determination will see you through. This is also a good time to take those classes you've wanted to take to develop your talents or to learn something new. Push yourself ahead.

Child

When this is your first challenge in life, you may feel repressed and have some resentment. You need to learn how to make your own decisions and to stand up for yourself. Your individuality is important. Realize that is what makes you unique from others, and don't try to be like anyone else. Instead, look for your own personal strengths. Some children naturally test their assertiveness as part of this Challenge.

THE 2 CHALLENGE: OVERCOME SENSITIVITY

During this cycle, your challenge is to face your own sensitivities and not take things so personally. Circumstances can make you emotional, so wait to make your decisions when you are not under emotional stress. This way you can face your problems without fear.

At times you feel you really want to please everyone and are so kind and sweet because you do want to be nice—but you are really uncomfortable around some of these clods. Use your innate good diplomatic manner, excuse yourself, and keep your distance from then on. You don't have to be a doormat to anyone.

You may have the habit of taking everything personally, letting little things bother you, and then holding grudges. You may allow people to take advantage of you and then resent it. This leads to unkind, thoughtless reactions. There are two things to remember in these situations: 1.) Realize that some people are so wrapped up in themselves they may not know that they may be hurting you; so forgive them and forget about it. 2.) Remember that no one is responsible for your happiness but you, so don't allow them to affect you emotionally. Only *you* can give other people power over you, and only *you* have the power to *not* let them affect you.

Realize that people will not always act or react the way that you expect. The only person you need to think about is you and the way you react to them. We can never control what others think or do, but we can choose how we react. A good thing to remember if we are confronted by an angry person is the Bible verse, "A soft word turns away wrath." It is so easy to bark back, but if we change that angry atmosphere with a soft kind word, the anger is diffused. So work to condition yourself to react with a calm voice in such situations. It will work wonders.

Another problem the 2 Challenge presents is disregarding details. Don't gloss over documents, legal papers, or small print.

Child

When this is the first Challenge, you will be very sensitive and take everything personally. You may feel insignificant and will try to imitate others. Once you discover your own talents and nurture them, you will start to develop your self-confidence and realize your own self-worth and the specialness of your individuality. The best advice to give a child is "be yourself."

THE 3 CHALLENGE: OVERCOME NEGATIVITY

This is the challenge of keeping a positive attitude and using the best side of your self-expression for a happier outlook. Opportunities can be lost because of a negative attitude and, strange as it may seem, many performers and professional people have this challenge to overcome.

It will help to develop your talents in order to become more self-assured, because, let's face it, you hate to be criticized. You will enjoy being sociable if you feel more worthwhile. This comes from creative hobbies, dancing, singing, writing, painting, or finding one area of interest and studying until you are an expert in it.

The secret for maintaining a positive outlook is to find the value in every negative experience and being grateful for having learned it. Everyone has a "best worst experience" to tell about, something that seemed awful at the time but resolved in a wonderful way that left them better off than before. Expect every bad experience to have a nugget of gold waiting for you, especially during this cycle when you tend to be too serious. Remember: Nothing bad lasts forever, so do your best to remain cheerful.

Look at the humorous side of things. Learn to laugh at yourself. It is surprising how much it lightens the load. Understand that you control every situation by your reaction, and it is your reaction that affects the outcome. The mature, well-balanced person is the one who has the control and is the winner every time.

Some who have this challenge spend too much money on unimportant things and then feel a need for it later. If money is a problem, take a course or read books on finance.

Your challenge may be that you talk too much, are a bore, or are a gossip. There is an old axiom, "If you can't say anything nice, don't say anything at all." If prone to gossip, imagine that person being nearby and hearing what you say. Embarrassing? Not only that, but anything we say about anyone has a way of getting back to them, and they will *know* it came from *you*. Once you realize the power of words and the joy that comes from using them to elate and lift people, you will have matured into that well-balanced person we all admire.

Child

As a first Challenge, you may be very shy as a child, finding it difficult to express yourself. There could also be a fear of personal criticism. Taking lessons to develop talents help to build self-confidence. Taking part in plays or joining a speech class can help immensely for personal expression.

THE 4 CHALLENGE: OVERCOME LAZINESS AND CARELESSNESS

This challenge of self-discipline is the easiest challenge of all. You simply have to learn to get organized and plan for long-term security. You have a tendency to put things off, be lazy, take shortcuts, and also mislay things. You are restless to accomplish something but have a difficult time getting started.

The best way to meet the 4 Challenge is to set goals for yourself and then make a schedule to meet those goals. Keep a diary to organize your thoughts at the end of each day. It may prove invaluable to you later when your memory is unable to supply accurate information.

Details are important! Get yourself a file and use it so you know where things are. Keep all your personal things neat and orderly. Make yourself do all the things that need to be done and do them thoroughly. Then reward yourself with leisure activities to your liking, for you tend to get into a rut and forget to take time to play.

You can be a little too straight-laced, set in your ways, and stubborn. Remember that some things take time, so don't try to force issues just because you are impatient. When things are right, they go easily for you; if forced, they cause more problems.

Don't let your strong opinions close your mind. Think fairly about the opposite point of view and perhaps a better way will open up to you.

It is always good to complete an education when in the 4 Challenge.

Child

As a first Challenge, you may be lazy, stubborn, and impatient. This is a time in your life when you must learn to organize your things and take the time to learn the importance of details. Develop good work habits while young, and take your studies seriously. Self-discipline will get you through many otherwise difficult struggles throughout life.

THE 5 CHALLENGE: OVERCOME IMPULSIVE ACTIONS

This can be the most difficult challenge, learning to use freedom wisely, which is to be responsible for your actions. You can't always do just as you please. Life will put temptations in your way and your natural urge will be to satisfy your impulses.

You are very sensual during this cycle and will want to try, test, and taste everything. Realize that complete freedom of action could prove detrimental to your health and future. Don't give in to all your desires that could lead to over-indulgence in any of the sensual things: drink, food, sex—anything that appeals to your mundane senses that could have negative results. And I guess we'll have to add drugs to that list—something we never had to think about when I was growing up and not something I would even consider a temptation, but now it is evidently an unfortunate available choice.

Make the Higher You take charge like a strong and gentle teacher, and learn to discern the difference between a restless desire to grow and one that purely wants to change. Remember: You don't have to try *everything*. Instead, observe others and take a lesson from their mistakes.

Another aspect of the 5 Challenge is that you must learn to discard what is no longer needed. This applies to conditions and concepts as well as clothes and, in some cases, people. Sometimes we let go of things too soon. So the lesson to learn is *when* to let go as well as *what* to let go. Don't do anything too quickly. Think before you act.

Child

As a first Challenge, you, as a child, are restless, are impulsive, and get bored easily. This is when you must learn to control urges and learn the true meaning of freedom, which is to be responsible for what you do.

THE 6 CHALLENGE: OVERCOME THE URGE TO CONTROL PEOPLE

There are times you feel that your efforts are not appreciated. You do more than your share and you know you do it better than anyone else, so you expect a thank you or praise. What you may not realize is that you tend to be very set in your opinions and feel that you are always right. And often you are, but what you may not be aware of is that you disregard *other people's* feelings. You may even find yourself doing the things you know they plan to do—or even redoing what they have done because you feel *you* can do it so much better. Can you imagine for a moment how you would feel under the same circumstances?

Sometimes in relationships or with family you give the impression that you feel you are so much better than they are. If you are smug, they feel it and resent it, and then you find yourself alienated from them. No self-righteous, smug person ever won a popularity contest, and as incredible as it may seem you *do* make mistakes. Come on, admit it. The fact is, it feels good to say, "I was wrong." People actually admire you for that. And when *you* show more appreciation, it is remarkable how much you are appreciated in return. It is far better for you to allow your family members and/or coworkers to set their own pace and express their own opinions. Remember that any issue that is forced will have negative results.

The tendency is to be too possessive. Take for your own the motto, "Live and let live." Really work hard to see others' points of view and allow them to do things their own way. Remember: People learn from their own mistakes. Let them spread their wings and grow. Their way may not be as good as *your* way, but it will certainly enhance your relationship with them and, at the same time, it actually takes a load off your back because the responsibility is no longer on your shoulders. There is no one more wonderful or more loved than a balanced and harmonious 6.

Child

When this is the first Challenge, the child either feels totally unappreciated, is overly stubborn and self-righteous, or looks down on others as being inferior. The need is to be loved and appreciated and to love and appreciate in return. If unhappy at home, you may marry much too young and later regret it.

THE 7 CHALLENGE: OVERCOME ALONENESS, LIMITATIONS, AND FEAR

During the time this challenge is in effect you will feel very much alone, even with people. You are very reserved and it is difficult for you to open up even to those close to you. It may be due to too much pride or something you feel is a personal or family embarrassment. You feel you want to just crawl away and hide, but at the same time you so much want to enjoy life and to learn something new to expand your awareness.

The challenge here is to forgive and forget past hurts and embarrassments and then find faith to go on with a happier attitude. Whatever you do, don't turn to drink. Go to your books. Take classes to improve your education, for then you will attract the best for you. Until you perfect your skills, you will feel limited and unhappy.

Seek to learn about the natural laws of the universe, spiritual laws. This will not only alleviate your fears, it will hone your intuitive skills and keep your focus on the positive side of life. One cannot remain positive and feel negative emotion at the same time. By remaining positive, a feeling of peace will well up from within and you will be able to accept life with a happy feeling and open arms, and your challenge will have been met.

Child

This is a tragic Challenge for a child. There is fear and embarrassment involved and the empty feeling of aloneness. Even if the child is in a good family, the child will need a great deal of support, to know it is loved, and to know that there is a loving God. There could be a health problem, isolation, or lack of education. Fortunately, this challenge is very rarely found.

THE 8 CHALLENGE: OVERCOME THE STRAIN FOR MONEY AND POWER

The 8 Challenge affects money matters, health, and personal values. It could mean money problems, or the desire for—or abuse of—power.

If your desire is for power, question your motives. Be sure your values are right or you could lose everything. Learn the rules of good organization so you become more efficient. Health could suffer for lack of proper nutrition or exercise.

If money is the problem it may be due to stinginess, wastefulness, or just not understanding finances and straining so hard for it. Part of this challenge is to learn how to handle money. During this cycle, you may be acutely aware of a feeling of limitation, yet there are wonderful opportunities waiting for you. Think more about *what* you love to accomplish rather than *how much* you will earn. By turning away from the feeling of strain and keeping your focus on your work, money will come easier for you and you could turn this challenge into a victory.

Also, the sense of limitation can be overcome by becoming philosophical. The study of Eastern and Western philosophies soothes the soul while helping us understand people and their different points of view. It gives us a deeper understanding of life, gets rid of a false set of values, and fills that empty void that causes the challenge in the first place. Once you have gained this knowledge, the feeling of strife will vanish and your mind will become peaceful.

If this is your final Challenge, learn management laws well so that *you* are in control instead of circumstances. Misuse of power will have hazardous results.

Child

If this is your first challenge, learn organizing skills and how to handle money wisely now, for this is the time you will be most receptive to it. Later on, without knowledge of finances, you may feel that money is the key to happiness and will make yourself miserable striving for it. There may be a desire or opportunity for power, so there is a need to establish good values now. Also, there is musical talent in this child that could possibly not be brought out until later years.

THE 9 CHALLENGE

There is no 9 Challenge possible because 9 is the highest number and cannot be subtracted from any other number. But there is a 0 Challenge that is quite common, and it is considered equal to the 9.

THE 0 CHALLENGE: OVERCOME INDECISION

When 0 is your Challenge, it does not mean that you won't have any problems, but rather that you should be better equipped to handle them. In order to make wise decisions you will need to know the basic law concerning the vibrations of all the Challenges. The following are the strengths needed to overcome them. Develop these and there will be no problem too difficult for you.

1 Will-power. Self-respect.
2 Self-confidence.
3 Self-expression. Cheerfulness.
4 Self-discipline.
5 Freedom and self-control.
6 Unconditional love.
7 Faith and understanding.
8 Right use of power.

Child

If the 0 is your first Challenge, you will have many an opportunity to make your own choices. A child can learn to make wise decisions by being taught how to weigh the pros and cons of any problem and guided to the right choice.

Part B: Opportunities

Our *Opportunities* come from inside us as urges and motivating forces that are longing for expression. They are energy fields, and we sense them when we begin to think in new directions. When we act on our new impulses or yearnings, we are using the energies within the vibration of the numbers that govern them. When we understand the qualities and traits of each Pinnacle's number (which is its rate of vibration), we have insight to the motives and urges that we must express in order to fulfill our destiny.

When a Pinnacle is the same as one of our major numbers, it is easier to fulfill our ambitions and dreams. But it is difficult when it is the same number as a Karmic Lesson that has not yet been learned.

In Chapter 2, you were shown how to find your Challenge and Opportunity numbers. The very top Pinnacle is your *Main Opportunity,* which means it stays with you throughout your life, not just in the last cycle where it is most dominant.

Again, with your chart before you, compare your numbers with the details that follow.

THE 1 OPPORTUNITY: PERSONAL ACHIEVEMENT

The 1 vibration always brings forth new experiences and the desire to use your pioneering spirit. All kinds of new ideas will thrill you to action. This is a wonderful time to get things done to your satisfaction and then start new projects. There will be many times you have the urge to take the initiative. And there will be chances to promote yourself and take the lead, just as you wish to do. Original ideas come easily, and you have the resourcefulness to act on them.

As a young adult, you may either find yourself on your own and having to support yourself, or may resist any helpful suggestions because of a feeling of self-importance. This is really the time to discover your leadership abilities and learn how to rely on yourself.

You may find that you are on your own due to either a change in marital status, your profession, or other circumstances. This cycle puts you on your own to learn to handle your independence without fear or having to lean on others. It is time to hone your latent abilities for creative thought, originality, and initiative.

Child

When this is your first Opportunity, everything revolves around you and your immediate family. Later on, it involves your circle of friends and acquaintances as well. You want to have your own way and do things yourself, and you are very stubborn about it. This is not easy as a first cycle because you want to be independent, and there is so much yet to learn in order to make wise decisions.

THE 2 OPPORTUNITY: PARTNERSHIPS AND COOPERATION

Three things are important for you to learn in this cycle: to overcome your sensitive feelings; the rewarding feeling that comes from being kind, gentle, and helping people; and practicing the patience that is necessary to do things carefully and accurately. The strengths to hone are patience, tact, diplomacy, tolerance, good will, and attending to details with accuracy and precision.

The 2 vibration has to do with getting along with people learning to share and to cooperate in a harmonious atmosphere. During this cycle, you may be called on to use your insight and tact in order to do so. This will involve your friends and family as well as your coworkers. At the same time, the sensitivities of the 2 are evident, so you must learn to deal with your emotions and not let them control you. Detailed work will appeal to you and you have the patience to do it well.

Child

As the first Opportunity, you will either be quite spoiled or overly sensitive and easily hurt. A child needs understanding and a great deal of love. If the parents are not aware of the child's inner fears and need of support, complexes can develop to make the child overly aggressive and hurtful to other children. The strengths waiting to be learned here are the spirit of cooperation and developing skills in any type of detailed work.

THE 3 OPPORTUNITY: EXPRESSING JOY AND CREATIVITY

This should be a happy time pursuing artistic events, socializing, developing your talents, writing, entertaining, and being entertained. Opportunities will present themselves where you can use your creative expression in singing, acting, any of the performing arts, writing, lecturing, even in decorating and designing—any of the creative arts you find stimulating.

Money should come easily in this cycle, but it will go as easily if you allow yourself to be careless. Negative circumstances can be avoided if you refuse to scatter your energies (and money is energy, too).

Your imagination is at its peak, making you creative and happy. So many good ideas are flowing that, should you be in a business that requires imaginative creativity, you will be most successful.

It is also a time to build lasting friendships where you really enjoy doing fun things together: taking walks in a park, or a trip somewhere, or even just walking your pets and enjoying the beauty of nature. You should feel free of worry and enjoy every day to its fullest. And you will, as long as you keep that rosy outlook.

Child

When this is your first Opportunity, you will want life to be fun and games all the time. Happiness is the whole point of living. There will be social events, many humorous happenings, and parties. It is also a time to discover your natural talents and to take lessons to perfect them. Its really important to develop your talents at this time or you could easily waste your time on frivolous things and regret it later on.

THE 4 OPPORTUNITY: WORKING FOR YOUR FUTURE

Four is the vibration of the honest achiever. Anyone in the vibration of 4 feels compelled to produce, to accomplish something rather than have fun and games. For the mature person, this is a very fruitful time period, but for one with a childish attitude or selfish concerns it can be the most difficult. However, much is learned in the process. You will develop organizational abilities and learn to work slowly and carefully, being extra attentive to details, gaining manual dexterity, and feeling a sense of pride for your work.

This is the time you think seriously about setting the foundation for your future, to work towards goals and for security. You will start a savings and look into speculations that pay you interest. This is also a family vibration and makes you feel the need to take responsible action for your family's best interest.

The 4 vibration is a practical one that wants to see results and is willing to plan and work hard to achieve the chosen goals. And you will gain determination, stick-to-itiveness, and a feeling of satisfaction for a job well done. If this is your last and main Opportunity, you may have this practical feeling throughout your life. And in your senior years you may, by necessity, need to work. But it could also mean having a worthwhile hobby that you enjoy that could bring in extra money—whether you need it or not.

Child

When the 4 occurs in the first cycle, it means you will have a job early in life. This is either due to necessity or the opportunity to lay the foundation for a chosen life's work. Either way, the feeling is clear that there is no time for play, but to work to free the self from limitations.

THE 5 OPPORTUNITY: CHANGE, ACTIVITY, AND FREEDOM

Each cycle is a duration of development. Five always denotes unexpected happenings and much activity. There is progress in spite of the restless feeling so often felt. It is time to test your adaptability. It could be a most happy and interesting period.

Now you will have the urge to travel, change jobs, or move. You feel ready for a change in your life, letting go of the old and welcoming the new. There will be many new experiences, some unexpected.

Because of the uncertainty of this vibration, there could be a fluctuation of income—very good at times and unstable at others. Don't enter into any legal ventures without forethought and complete awareness of all it entails.

As much as you love freedom and change, it is best to not do anything on the spur of the moment.

Child

This is not exactly a cycle of stability for a child, because it involves change, travel, and many activities. Either you moved a lot while you were growing up, or you traveled a great deal. This is a restless energy for a young person, and it involves many new experiences that may not be easy during youth, but helpful to draw upon in the future. The child must learn early to discard things no longer needed, to not be afraid of new experiences.

THE 6 OPPORTUNITY: DOMESTIC RESPONSIBILITIES

The 6 is always ready for responsibility: Home, family, and loving service are highlights. Six nurtures, soothes, and cares for family, friends, and community. Perhaps this is one of the reasons the 6 is known as the Cosmic Parent. The nurturing instinct is undeniably there.

This cycle will play host to either loving responsibilities or duties that burden you. But your nurturing nature will find a way to make the burdens lighter.

The 6 is also known as the voice that wants to be heard. For some there is the urge to use the voice for singing, for some to teach, and for others to voice opinions, perhaps by becoming involved in politics or community projects.

Another side of the 6 is the artist, the ability to redecorate and/or use the artistic abilities in other ways. You may have the urge to re-decorate a room or even the entire home. Some will buy special paint-ings or art objects; others will want to try to paint or make the objects themselves. The joy is in the creating.

Perhaps for you, this will be the opportunity to settle down and maybe get married. Chances are, you won't be lonely. This Pinnacle can bring fulfillment financially and personally.

If this is your last cycle, it is really a good vibration for retirement.

Child

If this is your first Opportunity, either it means living with the parents longer than planned or a shorter time than usual. It can also mean an early marriage.

THE 7 OPPORTUNITY: INTROSPECTION AND SOUL GROWTH

This is a quiet time for study and meditation. It is a period of self-contemplation when you will desire to better yourself through education and study. For some, it will mean scientific study. For a few it means perfecting one's talents. If this is you, you will demand excellence of yourself and will enjoy every moment of self-discipline to attain it.

You may sense an inner urging to look for deeper answers to the meaning of life. You want knowledge. You want to understand spiritual concepts. Your interests will peak in philosophy, theosophy, metaphys-ics, and/or esoteric sciences, and you will be in touch with your inner awareness to a much greater degree. Trips to the library or adding books of these interests to your own will fulfill an inner urging. Maybe you will prefer going back to school to gain new skills for a career.

There will be moments of restlessness and a feeling of waiting. To the undisciplined person there will be wide mood swings. But for the spiritually awakened, it can be a most rewarding time of personal growth.

This may be a difficult time if you are in a marriage where your mate is needing activity and togetherness—unless the spouse understands the ebb and flow of personal cycles. You must work at not being *cold and distant.*

Crowds won't appeal to you during this cycle. But nature walks, beautiful gardens, and scenery will appeal to you. You will really want more time to yourself and you will be highly selective about the company you keep. The 7 prefers to be alone or with like-minded people.

Child

This is a difficult period for you as a child. You will feel pretty much alone. Problems you may face are a family with too little money to provide the necessities, poor health, needing special education, having overly strict parents, difficulty making friends, and/or pressures in the home or school. On the brighter side, you may be the prodigy child whose interest develops very early in the study and perfection of a talent in music or sports, giving you little time for play.

THE 8 OPPORTUNITY: MATERIAL FULFILLMENT

Expect success! The 8 vibration is one of strength, courage, and good judgment. It gives a fine business sense, and you will desire to improve yourself in order to attain a higher position at work. There are ample opportunities for success during this cycle, and it is easily obtained unless your energies are scattered by either a lack of focus or an inability to control your emotions.

You may find yourself in charge of a work situation and/or real estate and possessions. It would be wise to learn budgeting and management, as there will be business expenses. You will have the inner desire to work hard toward your goals. Your ambition and strength should result in accomplishments that bring you material rewards.

It is not wise to place too much trust in other people unless you know or understand them. Serious problems can develop if matters of trust are put in the wrong hands. The 8 requires *your* attention to important matters. This is not an easy Pinnacle for a weak person, because it demands educated intelligence and the know-how of good management.

Child

If this is your first Opportunity, you may enter a profession very early in life. Sometimes it is because you already have the spark of desire to achieve in that area, or it may be that you *must* work in order to help support the family. In the latter case, you have a feeling of limitation and there is strain to attain.

THE 9 OPPORTUNITY: COMPLETIONS AND COMPASSION

The 9 is a high vibration that comes equipped with understanding, tolerance, and compassion. It is dramatic, romantic, and also highly impressionable.

The 9 favors the artist and actor in all of us and is very dramatic. This cycle is excellent for developing and using your personal talents as a hobby or a career. You are very impressionable at this time so it is wise to stay away from negative influences.

It is difficult to start new projects in this cycle because it is a time of completion. If, for example, someone gets married in this cycle, that marriage may not last, or, if a new job is begun, it may not be the last one.

Emotions will be high and there will be some disappointments, but they can be lessened by the good you feel in giving selfless service or just plain kindness and thoughtfulness, for the 9 loves people and finds great joy and satisfaction in uplifting their spirits.

This is a humanitarian vibration and the desire will be there to donate time and/or money to worthwhile projects and charities. But it is a very disappointing Pinnacle if all you think about is yourself. There could be a nice inheritance during these years.

Child

You came into the world loving everybody and were so dramatic and cute people couldn't help but adore you. You may remember hearing them say you must be an old soul. "Look at the wisdom in those eyes." Because the 9 is a vibration of completion, any long-term project may not last. This means that in the later part of the cycle when you are a young adult, you might marry and then divorce or separate. Or it could be that the first job is one that does not last. Although this is not a good time to start anything major, it is a good time to complete projects. One more thing of extreme importance: The 9 vibration makes people very impressionable. This child, especially, should not see any graphic movies or TV shows of a violent or sexual nature or be introduced to potentially deadly habits of drugs, smoking, or alcohol. They are damaging not only to the physical body, but to the psyche as well. Nightmares are common for these vulnerable and sensitive young ones.

THE 11 OPPORTUNITY: SPIRITUAL IILLUMINATION AND SENSITIVITY

This Master Number known as *The Psychic Master* is one that is artistic, spiritual, inspired, and a healer. During this cycle, you will have urges to better yourself and, because of your unusually keen intuition, you will intuitively know when opportunities are there for you. If you have followed these inner urgings and developed your talents, great success, awards, and even fame are in store for you.

You will feel either a heightened state of awareness or the depths of frustration, depending on your frame of mind and the extent of your education—which is important for the right opportunities.

Some will be drawn into the ministry, some into teaching, others into art. It is important to hold fast to your highest ideals, enjoy the finer things of life, grow spiritually, and set a good example for others. Keep this in mind when you have those moments of nervous tension, lack of patience, and frustration. And this does happen to many in the 11 vibration because of the strong desire for everything to be more perfect than it can be in your ideal world. Finding constructive outlets for your creative energies alleviates these negative conditions.

The 11 energy brings out the perfectionist in you. You can be so picky about certain things that it can make those near you uncomfortable. Realize that it is difficult for most people to live up to your ideals. If there are problems in relationships, they can be solved with tact.

Sometimes this vibration brings about a surprise ending of an association, partnership, or marriage. It may feel hurtful at the time, but it happens to draw one closer to spiritual thinking, philosophical study, and ultimately a deeper understanding of the self and of others. It is then a positive force for good in your life.

Child

The very first cycle is a personal period of development and, because 11 is a number of spiritual expansion and sensitivity, you, as a child, would be drawn toward religious or philosophical thinking early in life.

THE 22 OPPORTUNITY: MAJOR ACCOMPLISHMENTS

This Master Number, known as *The Master Architect*, is a very strong, energetic vibration that gives you the desire and ability to accomplish a great deal. You could achieve leadership status in a business or create something of great musical/artistic value.

Certain situations may involve you in very large endeavors from family and community to international affairs, for you care very much about the world as a whole and want to do your part to make it better.

This 22 energy makes you extremely sensitive and very much the perfectionist. It can be frustrating at times, but you will want to apply yourself until the job is done. Your practical approach is bound to get results.

Hold fast to your highest ideals and, with unselfish motives, seek to do the most for the greatest number of people.

If this comes in your last cycle, it is doubtful you will retire. You will be happier accomplishing something of worth.

Child

In a first cycle, this 22 energy will wear out the parents. This child wants to know how everything works: take the clock apart to see how it is made and then try to put it together again. If this was you, I hope your parents gave you lessons early to keep your little hands busy. A career could be born early if given the right education.

The Master Numbers

There are nine basic numbers. All the following compound numbers, 10 on, when added together, always return to one of the basic nine. However, there are several compound numbers that are considered numbers of mastery and are usually not reduced in numerology or astrology. It is said that these numbers are bestowed on "old souls" who are here to be of service to mankind. People who have these numbers prominent in their names or Birth Path are aware of a tremendous amount of nervous energy in their lives. Some can channel it into constructive projects that benefit many. Others use the energy in its negative aspect and never really realize their full potential. Others use the destructive side and cause great harm.

Children with Master Numbers have more nervous energy than other children and must be kept busy or given special projects to work on. It is extremely helpful for parents to know if their child's energy is due to the high vibration of their name or birth number.

People with these numbers do not always work in the high velocity of this energy or they would feel depleted in a short time. Instead, they often work and live in the root digit of the Master Number, but the achievement potential is always there.

The numbers considered to be Master Numbers are mainly 11 and 22. There are others: 33, 44, 55, 66, 77, 88, and 99, though these are rarely mentioned.

The 11 is the first and is the As Above, as is every alternate Master Number: 11, 33, 55, 77, 99. The others are the So Below: 22, 44, 66, 88.

The As Above numbers are more intuitive, psychic, and spiritually sensitive. The So Below numbers are better adapted to the material world. All are meant to be of service: the As Above in a spiritual or professional way, and the So Below in a material or physical way.

All Master Numbers are powerful because they accentuate themselves and their root number: 11/2, 22/4, 33/6, and so on.

THE MASTER NUMBER 11: THE PSYCHIC MASTER

All Master Numbers are filled with greater energy than single numbers because they include the vibration of the root number. The difference between 2 and 11 is that the 11 prefers to stand on its own two feet and take the lead rather than be the modest, willing follower that the 2 is. It has the natural abilities of the 1 and is artistic, spiritual, and inspired.

All 11s are meant to be professional people, for they cannot be happy in mundane work. Here are the inspired artists, painters, teachers, philosophers, ministers, musicians, composers, performers, and decorators. Their desire is to uplift others through the beauty of their creations or with their inspired thoughts.

They are an As Above number because of their highly intuitive and inspirational thoughts. They can mingle freely in the world and yet not be a part of it. They have a charisma, a mysterious glamour that makes them stand out in a crowd, and they easily draw followers.

The 11 is known as The Psychic Master—a messenger of God and a master among men, for it is the nature of 11 to delve into the mysteries of life. Jesus was such a master whose name total is 11. He desired to bring his light to the world, and *light* is the same numerical vibration. He said: "I am the *light* of the world. He who follows me shall not walk in darkness, but he shall find for himself the *light* of life" (John 8:12).

An 11 who does not pursue a spiritual or religious vocation is either artistic, musical, or politically inclined. Irving Berlin, who brought us hundreds of America's best-loved songs, was born on May 11th. An inspired pianist and brilliant entertainer who thrilled us with his performances was a man with a name totaling 11: Liberace. All 11s need music in their lives, and *music*, totaled by its letters' numbers also have the root of 11 (**M**-13, **U**-21, **S**-19, **I**-9, **C**-3). Add those: 13 + 21 + 19 + 9 + 3 = 65. Then add that total: 6+5= 11.

Elevens strive for perfection and will study hard to achieve it. They don't feel fulfilled unless they can give something to the world. Many become famous. On the other hand, they are easily disappointed in people, for they expect the same perfection in those they look up to. But those who are on the right path and find their success the darkness of confusion will be replaced with the light of understanding, and 11 will reflect that light. When that happens, we see the special glow, feel the charisma, and sense something special that radiates from the 11.

Negative 11s lack the practical aspect because they are not in tune with material matters. They become neurotic from not being able to make their brilliant dreams work for them on the material plane, and they have trials and hardship. The 11 warns of unknown danger, that there can be unexpected problems or trouble. The root of 11 is 2 and, like 2, they must learn to choose between good and evil, the opposite ends of the vibration. If there are two 11s in a name, the person may have very little tact.

Lower than that are the destructive 11s. Rather than lift humanity as the positive 11s do, these desire to rule and enslave others. They become despots, wicked leaders such as Hitler and Mussolini (name totals of 11), who were blinded by and misused their powers. Saddam Hussein is also an 11 name.

Eleven is significant because it represents duality.

Positive and NegativeTraits of Master 11

Positive

Inspired. Quiet. Reserved. Dignified. High ideals. Witty. Artistic leanings. Persuasive. Highly selective. Wants to uplift people (as a whole, not necessarily individually). Not a physical laborer, but a professional. May be religiously or politically inclined. Very creative. An excellent teacher.

Negative

Emotional. A daydreamer: It's far easier to dream about great things than to accomplish them. Represses feelings. Unfair. Prejudiced. Self-centered. Repressive leader. Aimless. Shiftless. Self-love. Miserly. A loner. Not at all practical. Expects too high a standard in others. Can't always put ideas into constructive form. Confused. In the world, but not a part of it.

Destructive

Lacks understanding. Extremely wicked. Dishonest. Devilish. Self-indulgent. Religious fanatics. May unconsciously antagonize others.

THE MASTER NUMBER 22: THE MASTER ARCHITECT, OR MATERIAL MASTER

Twenty-two is 11 + 11. It has the vision of the 11, but is able to put it to practical use. It completes work. It is very strong because it is the double of both 2 and 11.

Master Number 22 has always been the characteristic number of any circle, stemming from the fact that the original Hebrew alphabet consists of 22 letters that are the creative basis and attributes of all that has been created. So 22 represents the whole circle of creation.

As a So Below number, 22 makes manifest on the material plane. It is known as the Master Architect because it is capable of building the great roads, waterways, and buildings of the world. When working in the positive energy of this number, much good is accomplished. Many constructive ideas come to 22s and they have the innate ability to make their ideas reality.

The 22 knows how to unite the inspirational idea with the physical manifestation. Yet 22 is less spiritual than the As Above numbers 11 and 33. It is more adaptable to the earth plane; it can make manifest because of its root of 4. Plus, the 2 pays attention to detail and likes detailed work, so 22s are masters of detail.

The energy with this vibration is very high. In childhood, 22 is often hyperactive and must keep hands busy. This is the child who enjoys erector sets and building blocks and will try to take apart your favorite clock to see what makes it tick, and then attempt to put it back together again.

Because 2 is a number of sensitivity, 22 is doubly so. Safecrackers, whose unusually sensitive fingers pick up the inner clicks of the combination locks, have been found to have a strong 22 in their charts.

People with these Master Numbers in their name or birth date have an unusually high amount of nervous tension. This means potential for good, and when channeled into constructive projects they become the benefactors of society by building what is most needed by the people.

But those who become frustrated for lack of an outlet for these energies, either through lack of education or misguided direction, become a grave burden on society. Adolf Hitler is a prime example of a leader on the negative side of the Master Numbers. His total name is an 11 and he was born on the 22nd of the month.

Because of their nervous energy, 22s will have weak bodies and fragile health. They feel they must be constantly busy accomplishing something. The 4 root has a workaholic side to the vibration.

Positive and NegativeTraits of Master 22

Positive

Dynamic. Organized. Practical. A doer. A hard and tireless worker. Makes great achievements. A master of accomplishment. A very capable leader. An acute sense of touch.

Negative

Talks big. Feels inferior. Indifferent. Aimless. Fanatic. Service with ill will. Frustration. Nervous tension.

Destructive

Criminal. Extremely evil. Crooked. Black magic. Gang leader. On edge.

THE MASTER NUMBER 33: SELFLESS GIVING

This is the Master Number of spiritual giving. It is the As Above for it benefits the spiritual needs of others. The root number 6 is the vibration of home, love, family, service, and responsibility. The 33 goes a step higher by giving unconditional love.

The 33 doubles the attributes of the 3, vibration of joy and communication, love of children and pets, giving it a greater sensitivity to their needs, and pouring out a spiritual elixir of healing love. One who will do this is experiencing the 33 vibration. Jesus was 33 years old when he gave his life for humanity. The word *saviour* vibrates to 33, so this is known as the love vibration in its highest form: compassion.

Another aspect of the master 33 vibration is the experience of the Kundalini making its way upward through the 33 segments of the spine, opening the chakras as it rises, and causing a sort of spiritual orgasm—a tingling sensation throughout the entire body from the movement of the petals of each lotus-like wheel. When this force reaches the pineal gland (the Third Eye), the spiritual eye is opened and the initiate is ready for wisdoms to be revealed. From then on the person comes into conscious communion with the higher realms. In most people this spiritually energizing force lies dormant, and they experience only the strictly physical sexual climax.

Persons with 33 in a name or Birth Path number are highly sensitive to the needs of others, and through their occupations they will give of themselves in caring and comforting.

The 6 root represents the voice. When it is elevated to the 33 vibration we find it at its height in the great orator and inspiring teacher.

Positive and NegativeTraits of Master 33

Positive

Loving service. Compassion. Deep understanding. Selfless giving with no thought of return. Gentle. Kind. Unpretentious. Nurturing instinct. Empathetic.

Negative

Burdened. Careless. Sweet tooth. Shrill, unpleasant voice. Liar. Cheater.

Destructive

Martyr. A slave to others. Slovenly. Meddlesome.

THE MASTER NUMBER 44: MASTER THERAPIST

The 44 is the master who solves the material needs of the world. It is the So Below that makes manifest on the material plane.

Two 4s make this number doubly practical. Forty-fours are very resourceful. They can take valuable ideas and put them to work helping people build or rebuild their lives. Edgar Cayce provided solutions for seemingly unsolvable, insurmountable physical problems, and his Birth Path was 44.

Edgar Cayce did his work while under self-imposed *Hypnosis* (44). As his conscious self, his knowledge was ordinary. But when he had these *Tremendous* (44) *Encounters* (44) with his *Master-mind* (44) while in a trance-like state, his knowledge was *Unlimited* (44).

Dr. Jack Ensign Addington of the Abundant Living Foundation had a 44 Birth Path, and he gave spiritual insight, hope, and rehabilitation to countless prisoners and others through his radio ministry, "Peace, Poise, and Power," and *Abundant Living* magazine.

Dr. Addington was my minister when I was in college in San Diego in the late 1950s. *Minister*, by its letters' root numbers, is 44. Add that to his 44 Birth Path and we have the Master Number 88, a number of great success. The 44 is a very special kind of *Therapist* (44), one on a *Spiritual* (44) level. These people often have a foundation in *Theology* (44). See how all those words that vibrate to 44 are words somehow related and are of organized strength? The church throughout the ages has been a powerful *therapist* in showing how spiritual ideas can be used for our benefit.

Sometimes an extraordinary type of person will have a name that totals 44, such as the famous magician Houdini. His *Influence* (44) in illusion was such that people could not tell *Appearance* (44) from *Realities* (44), and with Houdini people were astounded with his incredible feats of illusion.

People with a 44 Birth Path or name total find themselves involved in helping themselves and others in physical or emotional therapy. It is a master commitment.

Positive and NegativeTraits of Master 44

Positive

A leader. Strength of conviction. Knows what needs to be done and how to do it. Confidence. Mental Control.

Negative

Overworked. Inconsiderate.

Destructive

Self-destructive.

THE REMAINING MASTER NUMBERS

These Master Numbers are rarely found in the name or birth date, but words that add up to these numbers correspond with the qualities of the numbers themselves.

The Master Number 55: Intelligence

The entire scope of all knowledge is contained within numbers 1 through 10. When they are added to each other their total is 55, so 55 is known as the number of intelligence. Because 5 + 5 =10, the number of perfection, 55 will strive for perfect answers. It is the As Above where perfection is reached.

Some words that total 55 are:

Numerology. Intelligent. Omniscience. Researcher. Aristocratic. Discipline. Profession. Dictionary. Orchestrated. Picturesque. Refinement.

The basic meanings of 5 are sexuality and the senses, freedom, curiosity, and adaptability, so the 55 is both a physical and a mental number. Its 10 root is a new start, on a new cycle.

Generations. Rejuvenation. Personality. Grandparent.

Some 55 words that have 100 as their full number are:

Lightning. Researcher. Discipline.

The 100 is the power of 10 raised to the cosmic level: 10 multiplied by itself. These are strong words. *Lightning* is unharnessed primal energy. *Discipline* makes us strong, and it is the *researcher* who finds the answers.

The Master Number 66: Creative Power

This is strictly an earthly vibration, the So Below where all is manifest in our three-dimensional world. There are six-dimensional aspects of matter as we know it: height and depth, right and left, back and front. This corresponds to the vowels of EARTH: **E**-5 + **A**-1 =6. So Earth's Desire (vowels) is to bring forth matter and to be our Cosmic Mother.

It is interesting that *woman* is 66 in its full number, and it is from the body of woman that the child is born. The 6 is known as the Cosmic Parent. The 66 is both father and mother, 6 + 6 is 12/3, and 3 is the child. So 66/3 is father, mother, and child, and the 12 preceding the 3 represents the 12 signs of the Zodiac.

The Master Number 77: Christ-Consciousness

The 77 is known as the number of the Christ-consciousness because *Christ* has 77 as its full number, and Jesus was the 77th in his line of ancestry. Related words that total 77 as the full number are:

Disciple. Power. Glory. Stars. Abundant.

True 7s are spiritual. The more spiritual, the more they radiate that *"spiritual-quality,"* an *"intensification"* of inner wisdom. (*Spiritual-quality* and *intensification* total 77 and are in that rate of vibration.)

The Master Number 88: Success

The master numbers 88 and 99, I have found, exist in words by their full totals only.

The 88 is a number of the Master Executive, one who has met with tremendous success. It is an As Below, or physically manifest vibration. The 8 is a picture of the cycle of all life, and success is due to continual application of the governing laws. By full word total it has such words as:

Pianist. Excellence. Exercise. Vision. Apostle. Proper. Dignity. Agreement. Pleasant.

To me it is particularly interesting that *Pianist* should have the full number of 88, for the instrument played has 88 keys, and anyone who has mastered this remarkable instrument has certainly reached tremendous success.

8 + 8 = 16/7. Seven is the root that represents analytical study, spirituality, and perfecting the self.

When the mind is kept on a purely physical level it becomes *poison* to the body (poison's full word total is 88). But when consciousness is raised to the spirituality of the root, 7 (88/16/7), the great power of the double 8 blossoms forth in the full-fledged *Apostle* with his *Vision,* the *Pianist* who reaches *Excellence* through *Exercise*, and all is *Proper* and *Pleasant.*

The Master Number 99: Fulfillment

The 99 represents complete fulfillment. By full word total it has such words as: *Accomplish. Satisfy. Comforted. Ascension. Poetry. Thought. Fortune. Answers. Physics.*

The ninth letter is I. So 99, or Ii, is the I of the Higher Self and the i of the ego. When the ego is in tune with the Higher Self, complete fulfillment is possible.

The Testing Numbers

There are four numbers that can be warning signs for you: 13, 14, 16 and 19. They have been called *Testing Numbers, Warning Numbers, Malefics,* and *Karmic Debt Numbers,* for they can symbolize payment demanded for wrong deeds in a past life time. These particular numbers have been found to be stronger in their negative and positive aspects than any other numbers. They are found in your chart only as totals in the major name numbers (vowels, consonants, vowels and consonants combined) and birth date (total of month, day, and year, not the birth day alone), so don't confuse them with the numbers missing in your name or anywhere else on your chart.

The numbers themselves are the adjectives that describe their root, which is the clue to the way the test should be handled: The 1 in each case is the self. The number following it is the clue to the energies misused in a previous life. And the root is a clue to the way the debt can be resolved in this life. Plus, the corresponding letter to the root number gives us deeper insight into solving the problem and passing the test. Let's look at them separately.

13: CONSTANT CHANGE.

Must be dedicated to a purpose.
Past error: Laziness.

Change is constant in man physically, emotionally, and mentally, and change is the deeper meaning of 13/4. There are some problems you would rather not deal with because of the negative *emotion* involved. You, the 1, will want to hide in your 3, travel away from the problem, and just enjoy life (having fun or just being lazy) in the 3 energy. But the root, 4, while making you feel limited, will force you to face the problem squarely by becoming *mentally* involved and taking the necessary *physical* action.

The negative side is realized when the carelessness of the 3 gives in to the strong negative will of the 1.

The positive side of 13 is attainment (4), where there are unlimited powers for creating something of lasting value.

Our 13th letter, M, is called Mem in Hebrew, meaning water, and to the ancients water represented the emotions. Our M is drawn to reflect those up and down waves of water. It is the only letter that is sounded with the mouth closed; mute, so the ancients called it the letter of death. But to them death meant change, not finality. Whenever a change takes place, the old is gone, dead, and the new emerges from it. Often it is a welcome change. Esoterically, it means the death of a man as a mortal and his rebirth as a disciple reaching for higher consciousness. This is the true meaning of 13: the death of the old material self and embracing spiritual laws for soul growth and a higher awareness.

14: TEST OF THE SENSES

Must seek to be wise.

Past error: Undisciplined physical appetites.

The 14/5 is known as *The Great Destroyer,* a malefic Testing Number for it pays back whatever is put out and causes one to learn from experience. You, the 1, must learn the honesty and integrity and the discipline of the 4 in order to handle the freedom-loving 5.

The root, 5, is the middle of numbers 1–9 and is known as the number of man, for man has five physical senses. In the undisciplined man, these senses want to be overindulged in self-gratification, with physical passions such as food, drink, drugs, and sex. These can be *Great Destroyers* of health and relationships. The negative side of 5 also brings separations, disappointments, and restlessness. The 14 always learns through experience, for it is impulsive, acting without consideration of consequences.

Yet the positive side is equally powerful. This number proves the power of thoughts, for 14 is composed of two 7s, and 7 is the vibration of mental perception and analytical ability. From this double 7 energy, 14 gets the power to overcome sensual temptations and to use the mental skills for soul growth (another dimension of the 7 vibration), so the 14 contains positive help for the negative aspects of 7.

Our 14th letter N in Hebrew is also N, and called Nun, meaning fish, but numbered as 50 (same root of 5). Its significance here is in the deeper symbolic meaning of fish. The sea where fish swim represents the depths and fullness of our consciousness, and the fish are the esoteric truths that must be caught and consumed in order to have them become a part of our conscious awareness. Thus, fish symbolize the realization that comes with deeper understanding. When the 14 gains this wisdom and becomes wise, it will have won the test of the senses.

16: WARNING TO BE CAREFUL—WATCH THE WORDS

Must seek spirituality.

Past error: Unsanctioned love.

The warning of 16/7 to be careful has to do with having love affairs where you are the *other* man or woman, one where someone is bound to get terribly hurt because of your involvement. This was an error in a past life and the opportunities will continue to arise in this life to test you.

The 1 refers to the self that cares for its body. The 6 represents the physical body and the voice needed to speak the right words. This meaning came from the Biblical account of man being created on the sixth day and the fact that everything in our three-dimensional universe, including our body, has six sides: front and back, top and bottom, right and left.

In the past, the body and/or voice was misused, and strictly material living was ruinous to the health. The 7 root gives its power of thought through analytical ability and its innate spiritual sense, to realize the results of one's actions and to think well before starting a ruinous chain of events in this lifetime.

Our 16th letter, P, corresponds with the Hebrew letter Pé, mean-ing *mouth*. Wrong words can ruin us. The mouth is used to eat, and wrong food can also harm us. Physically, this letter in Hebrew refers to the left ear, indicating the importance of what we hear. That is, everything we hear is food for the mind, and both good and bad are impressed on living tissue. And so, the number 16 cautions us to pay close attention to what we say, what we eat, what we hear, and what we do. We can fall slaves to our weaknesses and addictions or assume power over our thoughts and habits, becoming masters of our own destiny. When lived rightly, the 16 expression is healthy, artistic, cre-ative, and successful.

19: INITIATION

Test of emotions and spirituality. Unselfish goals and independent spirit.

Past error: Misuse of power.

In 19/1, the 1 is the self. The 9 is everyone else. The root is 1, the self again. Translated, the 1 uses power over the others for selfish gain—thinking only of how it can use others for selfish reasons. It may be in a past life you took undue advantage of people. This was a misuse of personal power that you will be tested on in this lifetime.

The 9 is not just other people, it is the emotional and dramatic part of you. The number 19 gives a sense of urgency. Situations arise that force you to stand on your own two feet. There are tests and initiations: the self (1) finishing lessons (9) in order to reach comple-tion/perfection (1+9=10). All karmic debts are brought to a head.

The 9 is also a vibration of brotherly love, caring for other people. So part of this initiation is to become less concerned with referring everything to the self and actually putting other people first. The moment the realization comes that caring about others gives you a warm and wonderful response, there will be no turning back to selfish ways. That caring feeling gives so much more satisfaction.

Our 19th letter is S, the Hebrew equivalent of Samech (60) mean-ing prop or bow (the bow that sends the arrow). The spiritual mean-ing is *The Law of the Circle;* whatever we send out returns to us, what we sow, we reap.

The actual 19th Hebrew letter, Qoph, applies here too. Qoph means "back of the head," the area of coordination and balance. The Hebrew letter itself, ÷, resembles a profile. The back of the head being at the right is significant, for their belief was that the left faces God. This is why Hebrew is written from right to left: They are always going towards God to "blend our consciousness with that of God," another meaning of Qoph. And one last meaning is that of mirth, which is another great balancing power. In fact our Q was drawn to look like a head with a tongue sticking out to represent mirth. Many stressful situations have been eased with a good sense of humor. Humor is well appreciated as one of the strongest aids in healing.

All these things are clues as to how to pass this test of karmic debt.

Understanding Your Child

No two children are alike, so it is helpful to make a numerology chart for your children so you can see what their particular needs are. Although all the points on the chart are revealing, I have found the Total Expression to be most helpful in knowing how best to handle them. Remember that this tells all their talents and potential. That, again, is the full name number of combined vowels and consonants. Once you have your child's number of the complete Birth Name, read the matching number in the following pages and you will find the main temperament and needs.

A CHILD'S TOTAL EXPRESSION

1 children

One children are very bright and quick-witted. They are leaders, not followers, so it is wise to give them direction early in life. When taught *why* one alternative is better than another, they will grasp that idea and use it their advantage.

Never bark orders to 1 children. They resent being told what to do. They are individual, creative, and need only be directed in the right way. Led properly, these children can grow up to be good leaders.

Without guidance, these children think only of themselves. They will bully other kids, boss them around, form gangs, and instigate mischief. So it is wise to give 1 children vocational training while young.

They love doing something individual, and it gives them a natural self-esteem.

Teach these children the importance of kindness and consideration toward others. One is a mental number, and they will become bored if there isn't something to occupy their mind. Find suitable games that they can play alone or with others that stimulate that little mind to learn.

One children must develop body, mind, and spirit to the highest point of efficiency. The need is to acquire a feeling of friendliness and affinity for people.

Positive attributes: Creative. Individual. Original. Courageous. Determined. Leadership.

Negative traits: Aggressive. Boastful. Egotistical. Impulsive. Pushy. Know-it-alls. Smart-alecks.

2 children

These children have so many charming qualities: sweetness, helpfulness, easy-going, quiet, and cooperative. They love to please others and need the warmth of praise and love in return. They are quiet children who can sit for hours with their books, games, and puzzles, for they have great patience and don't get bored easily. They will enjoy hobbies, especially collecting things.

Two children enjoy companionship, a playmate, or a pet or two. They don't mind sharing a room and are considerate of another's possessions.

The 2 is an emotional vibration, so these children can be overly sensitive; they may cry a lot. It is important to establish in them a sense of self-worth. Let them know that their ideas and feelings count and that they are loved. Because the 2 is an eager follower, see to it that more forward children do not mislead them.

They do not want to be leaders or be in the limelight. Group participation classes, such as dancing, chorus singing, and group sports, are far more comfortable than training for any type of solo performance.

These children should never be in an environment of vulgarity and crudeness. This wars with the tender inner nature and can cause instabilities in character.

Praise them often for their efforts. Make them realize their self-worth and they will be far less likely to be influenced to follow any negative peer pressure. All 2s need a purpose to pursue.

Positive attributes: Peacemaker. Cooperative. Sincere. Persuasive. Sensitive and caring. Natural insight. Tact and diplomacy.

Negative traits: Self-consciousness. Timidity. Unhappiness. Moodiness. Prone to steal. Deceitful.

3 children

Precocious. These children will amuse and entertain you, do cute things to make you laugh, and perform to hear your applause, for 3 children are meant to be givers of joy. They have personality plus if not stifled by parents who become annoyed with what they see as a child needing constant attention, and then squelching it.

These children need creative outlets, for they have much artistic talent just waiting to be nurtured. Painting, drawing, and crafts can keep 3 children happily busy. They love parties and are often the life of it. These children can be quite an asset as a little host/hostess for your dinner parties at home. There are certain responsibilities a child can handle very well, and each one learned will lighten your load.

Be sure to give them music lessons, dancing, and singing, anything that will further develop their natural knack for entertaining. When older, they may enjoy creative writing, acting, debate teams, and public speaking. You will never be sorry you gave them lessons to bring out talent for self-expression. Those lessons will lay the foundation for future progress, success, and happiness. All 3s need to acquire concentration and stick-to-itiveness, and having lessons at an early age set good habits for life.

Positive attributes: Happy. Artistic. Creative. Inspired. Imaginative. Joyous.

Negative traits: Moody. Critical. Selfish. Gossipy. Scatters energies. Holds grudges. Talks too much.

4 children

These children are very serious; they want and need to be governed by rules and regulation. They must know where their boundaries are. That way they feel secure. They appreciate being shown a method for accomplishing things, for they have an innate need to be organized.

They must not be hurried. They want to take their time to do things at their own pace, and do them well. A hurried 4 is a harried 4.

Four children love to build things from baby building blocks to erector sets. Musical instruments requiring manual dexterity, such as the piano, organ, violin, trumpet, or guitar, all appeal to these children. They will enjoy studying and practicing to perfect technique, and even prefer it to social involvement because they take to self-discipline. They are very good with their hands, artistic or mechanical.

These children need a lot of love, but are naturally so straight-laced that they find it hard to show appreciation for it. When parents realize the children are not cold, but inhibited, it is easier to deal with that attitude. Just continue loving and praising these children for jobs well done. These 4 children have a deep, loving response within that doesn't always show, but it's there.

Positive attributes: Practical. Determined. Moral. Honest. Conscientious. Patriotic. Powers of concentration.

Negative Traits: Opinionated. Stubborn. Too serious. Argumentative. Narrow-minded. Material. Vulgar.

5 children

These children are charmers, with outgoing personalities. They will be popular with classmates because of their charisma and carefree attitude. This personality is multifaceted, clever, quick, fun, and daring. In fact, they will sell more cookies for the school than any other.

Five children are not always easy to handle because of their innate curiosity that gets them into everything. They won't sit still for long and get bored easily, so they always need something to do.

Teach these children a moral code early. Otherwise female 5s are the first to get pregnant, and male 5s the first to be fitted with a paternity suit. You see, the 5 mind must be guided and directed well, for the 5 vibration represents the five physical senses that must try, taste, and test everything. Couple that with curiosity, and you have your hands full.

Another valuable lesson to teach 5 children is when to discard no longer useful items, for they usually hold on to things too long. And trips? Oh yes! They love to travel. They want to see the world and learn all about it. They learn languages easily, too.

In school these children will excel in the things that interest them. Period. When bored in class, their minds will wander off to things more exciting. They need training and a good education or they will drift through life with a lack of discipline. Early training instills patience, a quality that must be learned. When given a good foundation, 5s grow up to be very successful, happy people.

Positive attributes: Adaptable. Versatile. Energetic. Curious. Outgoing. Love of life. Charming.

Negative traits: Too willing to try everything once can lead to self-indulgence in bad habits. Restless. Discontent. Moody. Bad temper. Impulsive. Dissatisfied. Addicted. Impatient.

6 children

Family is very important to these children. They need roots, a home, and adoring parents. Six children are mature beyond their years. They want responsibilities and do them well, and they may even think of better ways to do them. And when they do, praise them, for they have great need to feel appreciated.

Pets are important to these children. They need something to dote their love on. To tend and care for a pet fulfills their nurturing instinct. If you don't want a dog or cat, birds make wonderful pets. I grew up with canaries and parakeets, and they are very lovable. They may be small, but they show great love for their owners.

These children are not at all "A students," for they are not naturally studious. But they try and do well enough because they really want to. They need to know you are aware of that, for approval matters to them.

They love being at home, and you'll usually find them playing happily with their friends in their own room or backyard. They like to play at "my house." Having their own room means more than you know. They have this instinct for responsibility and enjoy keeping things nice in their space.

Girls will enjoy learning how to bake. At as early as six they can put ingredients together to help Mom. With supervision, they can do much more. Don't forget to compliment them on doing a good job. That is their reward, and they need that.

Six children like to know the rules and live by them. It really upsets them to see people disregarding established laws, and these children worry about that. They want to see the law upheld because it makes them feel more secure.

They have artistic and creative talents and a natural love for beautiful things. When they are old enough, allow them to select the colors and decorative objects for their own room. Aesthetic surroundings are important to their nature.

Positive attributes: Cares for others. Loving. Kind. Open and honest. Unselfish. Domestic. Artistic. Idealistic. Willing to serve.

Negative traits: Anxiety. Stubborn. Self-righteous. Obstinate. Smug. Bossy. Interfering.

7 children

These children seem wise beyond their years. Don't worry if they prefer to play alone, for 7 is a mental vibration and these children must have time alone with their thoughts. They need a room of their own where they can study, play, and dream. They will have one or two well-chosen friends, for they prefer a quality relationship to a quantity of acquaintances. They may even have an imaginary playmate.

They should do well in school, for they love books and study and have the power of concentration. These fine qualities may out-picture as being quiet and secretive, but in truth, they are reserved in manner and are deep thinkers. They strive for perfection.

They want and need love. They keep their feelings locked inside, and, as long as you are aware that they are not naturally demonstrative, and that they do love deeply and appreciate the love they are shown, the easier it will be to understand them.

Very young 7 children should be given toys that stimulate the mind. They will take to scientific things and will want to find out how things are put together.

This child may have bad dreams and be frightened to be alone in the dark at night, so be sure they have a night light so the room won't be so terribly dark. All 7s need faith, to know there is a loving God. This should be nurtured early in life, for it fills an important inner need. They will be drawn to philosophical things and need to overcome fear and loneliness.

These children are fussy about food. Don't force them to eat everything. Well, that's good advice for any child. We all have our tastes and to have to eat something Mommy and Daddy like is sometimes gut-wrenching for a child. I know for myself, I couldn't stand even the smell of asparagus when I was young, and now I just love it. Let's face it, our tastes change. Some foods appeal to adult tastes. So never force children to eat something when they aren't ready for it. They will never turn down something they like. Right? I must add this. I have three children. One liked only vegetables, one fruit, and the other bologna. I often said that, among them, they had a balanced meal. However, they are all grown now and always have been very healthy. So it isn't necessary to force children to eat what they don't want.

Seven children usually have good self-control, but when so much builds up inside they will erupt with a temper tantrum. If there is a problem to be talked out, 7s must do it when they are ready and not until then. Speak your piece. Then leave them alone to mull it over. They will come to you when they are ready to talk.

Positive attributes: Observant. Cautious. Analytical. Dignified. Discriminating. Intelligent. Inventive. Charming.

Negative traits: Cynical. Sarcastic. Shrewd. Suspicious. Argumentative. Bad temper. Unreasonable. Repressed. Too much pride. Fear.

8 children

These children have innate musical talent. It is wise to start them with piano lessons, the basis of all instruments. Eight is a mental vibration and needs mental stimulus. Music lessons train the hand and mind.

These children are natural savers; they may start collecting pennies and then move on to big change. They may not want to put it in a bank though, because they like to take it out and count it to see it is all there and growing. When they are older, they will appreciate a savings account. Encourage them to save for special things, and then see the joy in their eyes when they buy it themselves. This will set a firm foundation for wise spending for the future. Your little 8s will come up with all kinds of ideas to make money and will suggest, organize, and run a lemonade stand or garage sale efficiently.

These children are leaders, and can influence other children. It is important to guide them during the formative years so this talent for power is directed in positive ways. A good spiritual background will balance out their character and accentuate all their natural, good qualities.

These children have a lot of physical stamina and this can be directed into physical activity, such as sports or dancing. Many 8s become successful athletes and go into business later in life. They will make fine executives some day.

Positive attributes: Physical strength. Capability. Executive ability. Good judgment. Efficient. Organizational skills.

Negative traits: Tries too hard. Tense. No humanitarian feelings. Overly ambitious.

9 children

These children have high ideals and deep emotions, and they may tend to be moody. It is important to draw out the innate creative talents so they can find fulfillment in artistic expression. Singing, dancing, learning to play a musical instrument, and participation in sports are all good outlets for their abundance of energy. So are responsibilities such as having a pet to love and care for, or a garden to work in, things that don't require a rigid schedule.

Let these children know they are special to you. Their individuality is important, and they should be encouraged to develop their natural abilities in order to know themselves. This is because the 9 is impressionable. Unless they find their individual strengths early, they tend to follow their peers. It is very difficult for 9s to break a habit once it is begun. They need encouragement and a good education in order to realize their full potential.

Home and family are important to 9s. They love to be surrounded by things of beauty and take interest in the furnishings and decorative touches. They have a talent for putting colors together.

These children in particular are very easily influenced. Be careful and selective in the movies they see. They take on the "spirit" of the message and it is hard to throw it off. Also, it is important for them to know they are unique and that they should be themselves. I remember a wise adult telling me when I was very young that I should never try to be like anyone else because I had my own unique talents. "Be true to yourself." Those are especially important words today when so many young people try to be like the current pop star—not a worthy achievement at all.

There is an inner wisdom in a 9 that radiates as charm and warmth. They are so deeply emotional. These are the children that will take your face in their hands when you cry and say, "What's wrong, Mommy? Can I make things better?" Such human compassion makes them very special indeed.

Positive attributes: Loving. Understanding. Forgiving. Charitable. Idealism. Perfection. Compassion.

Negative traits: Self-love. Depression. Possessive. Wrong habits. Impulsive.

11 children

These children love to daydream, may have an imaginary playmate, get lost in their own thoughts, and may not hear you call.

When these children are interested in something, they will learn about it quickly and easily. They refuse to concentrate on anything that doesn't mean anything to them, so you don't have "A students" here except in subjects they care about.

Give them lessons in art and acting. They express themselves so well in creative ways. Their imagination knows no boundaries. Developed right, they can grow to be community leaders, inspired teachers, well-known actors, or dynamic preachers.

Don't push 11 children into any kind of business career. They are inspired, not practical. Nurture their creative abilities and let them blossom at their own pace, and you will be proud of them.

Eleven is a Master Number. Its energies are at a very high level and can be difficult to live up to. These higher energies are meant to inspire and give selfless service to humanity. Many 11s live mainly in the base vibration of 2 (1+1=2). Twos are cooperative and kind, but they lack leadership that 11s possess. Children sense this power at an early age. This is why it is important to seek out their natural artistic talents and develop them so they can tap into their inborn intuition that leads to inspiration. All 11s are happiest when they can work with their creative abilities in order to uplift and inspire others.

On the negative side, the 11 energy is most destructive. Instead of leading gently, they misuse their power to rule tyrannically. These children have the potential for great good or great evil—depending on how they are nurtured and guided. It is the difference between a Jesus and a Hitler (both are 11s).

Positive attributes: Intuitive. Idealistic. Inventive. Artistic. Spiritual.

Negative traits
Needy. Miserly. Dishonest. Self-indulgent. Tyrannical. Liar.

22 children

These are charming, loving children with magnetic personalities. Their eyes seem full of wisdom, and you can't help but feel there is greatness there.

These children have big plans early in life and are full of the energy to carry them out. They need to be kept busy with worthwhile activities, or their natural drive could go into less desirable projects. These are the children that see your favorite clock and, when you aren't looking, will take it apart to see what makes it tick, and then try to put it together again.

This is a Master Number with great inherent power. It is sometimes called the "Material Master," for they can get ideas on an inspirational level and put them into practical use on the material level for the betterment of humanity. Even as children, 22s can find practical solutions to problems that others find impossible to solve.

These children keep pretty busy on their own. Choose games that are mentally stimulating and constructive. Encourage the intellectual proclivities: If they are interested in science, get them a telescope, microscope, or chemistry set. If they are interested in putting things together, be sure there are building blocks, erector sets, and, later on, model planes, ships, cars, and so forth. These minds want to put ideas to practical use for a reason not yet apparent.

Being double 2, they are very sensitive. Don't say anything negative about them that they can hear. It will devastate them. Of course, this is true for any child. Those little ears believe everything they hear about themselves and will live up to or down to that belief that has just been instilled in them.

The 22 is a stronger mind than body. Be certain this child has healthy eating habits.

Positive attributes: Charming. Personality plus. Concentration. Application. Loving.

Negative traits: Cunning. Conniving. Deceitful. Destructive. Vicious. Cruel. Sneaky. Liar.

Chart 7:

George W. Bush
7-6-1946/ 33

<pre>
 5 6   5 *1   5   3   = Soul's Urge 25/7
GEORGE WALKER BUSH
7   97   5   32   9 2   1 8 = Personality 53/8
</pre>

Inner Guidance **3**

Expression **15/6**

Golden Goal **3**

Birth Path **33**

- -

Raised W

<pre>
 5 6   5 51   5   3   = Soul's Urge 30/3
GEORGE WALKER BUSH
7   97   *   32   9 2   1 8 = Personality 48/12/3
</pre>

Inclusion Table								
1	**2**	**3**	**4**	**5**	**6**	**7**	**8**	**9**
2	2	2	--	4	1	2	1	2
A	B	U	--	E		O	G	H	R
S	K	L	--	E			G		R
				E				
				W				

Karmic Lesson **4**

The Planes of Expression
Physical - **4** EEEW
Mental - **3** ASH
Emotional - **5** BKULO
Intuitive - **4** GGRR

	Challenges	Age	Opportunities	
	1	Birth to age 30	4	
	4	30 - 39	8	
	3	39 - 48	11	
Main Challenge	5	48 - on	9	Main Opportunity

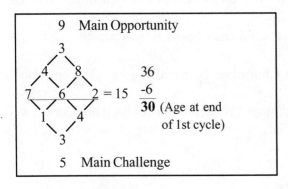

9   Main Opportunity

```
        3
      /   \
    4     8        36
   / \   / \       -6
  7   6   2  = 15  ____
   \ / \ /         30  (Age at end
    1   4              of 1st cycle)
     \ /
      3
```

5   Main Challenge

Chart Analysis of President George W. Bush

GEORGE WALKER BUSH

Now you have all the keys for personal discovery and should have found it easy to make and read your own chart and perhaps learned a little more about yourself on the journey. When you know the Birth Name and date of others, it will now be easy for you to see into their characters. This is no guessing game. Just tell what the numbers mean. Of course, good people and bad all share the same numbers; they just live at the opposite end of the vibration. When it comes to character, we choose to be positive, negative, or destructive.

When you read charts for people you don't know, tell them the positive and negative sides of their numbers. They love to discuss it with you, and you can learn so much from this. It is easier yet to chart a well-known person. What you don't know about them you can read in their biography and you will see how they really do reflect their numbers.

Just for fun and clarification, we are going to do that right now. I chose President George W. Bush because he is an important figure in our world at the beginning of our 21st century, and also because he has that W, so you can see how that double Soul's Urge works in his life and how that also affects his personality and the way he likes to dress. You can refer to his chart at the beginning of this chapter as we go along. (The biography I refer from is *W: Revenge of the Bush Dynasty* by Elizabeth Mitchell.) You can refer to his chart at the beginning of this chapter, and the explanations of those numbers in Chapters 3 – 9.

175

GEORGE WALKER BUSH: July 6, 1946

George Walker Bush became the 43rd president of the United States in January 2001 after being the 46th governor of the state of Texas. There he earned the reputation of being a compassionate conservative. His beliefs are limited government, strong families with personal responsibility, and individual states having local control.

Because the W in President Bush's middle name adds a delicate "oo" sound to Walker, it is considered a semi-vowel and shows its influence by giving a second major Soul's Urge at some time in his life. I originally expected this second desire to become manifest when a person was older, but I found with George W.... it was active along with his first desire since boyhood. Either way, the double desire does make the life and personality a bit more colorful, as we shall see with President George W. Bush.

With W as a consonant, his first desire is 7, as a vowel it is 3.

I. Soul's Urge or Desire

The 7 Soul's Urge, or Desire: The Thinker

In pilot training George W. was one of the very few who easily read charts on the functions of planes. He could sift through the data and consider it analytically. The class had to memorize the entire make-up of the plane, and it came easiest to George W. because he could commit information to memory, a habit he got into when his dad had him and his brothers commit baseball cards to memory when he was just a boy.

George W. has the gift of connecting with people, making them feel comfortable and happy, a trait more important than any academic classes he took in college. Those who know him say he has great charm and a twinkle in his eye. As a boy, George W. had many friends. He said himself that the biggest difference between him and his father was that they went to different high schools: George Sr. in a wealthy New York suburb and George W. in Midland, Texas. Whereas George Sr. had a chauffer take him to and from school, George W. walked, rode his bike, or was dropped off by his mother, so he led the school life of the average middle-class American schoolboy. Although his dad was known as a great communicator, George W. really understood the people, and his greatest strengths are his personal charm and stamina.

George W. arrived at Andover in 1961, all of 15 years old. It was a very strict school, difficult and serious for a young boy. They were forced to do difficult physical things such as climb a rope ladder three stories high and then shimmy down a cable (for fire drill practice) and, worse yet, have their hands tied and be thrown into a pool as the faculty watched them struggle to keep from drowning. He fell back on his wit in order to cope with the situation and it earned him the nickname "Lip." He learned the "sharp-edged" tongue from his mother, and he used it to get a point across without being disrespectful. He was never cruel and never wanted to hurt anyone. He learned from his father that it does no good to slam anyone, and he always greatly respected his father.

At Yale, his friends called him "Little George," and he got along well with all of them. But there were a few in his last years there who were intellectual snobs and name-droppers who treated him with disrespect by attacking the political positions his father had taken. That hurt, and George W. took that personally, so he was quite aloof and distant with people like this.

George W.'s dad was a great baseball enthusiast and taught his boys very early to love the sport. He took them to games and played catch with them in the backyard. Soon, George W. was enjoying playing the game himself. They say that because of his height he was usually the catcher. He didn't mind because that had him in most every game. Even his mother was involved by keeping score, which she had done during her husband's days at Yale when she was pregnant with George W.

Behind the 7 Root: Leadership

Here we see the influence of the adjective numbers behind the 7. Robert Birge, a friend of his, said, "I've always admired his ability to interact with people and his effectiveness at getting his point across. He does it with an intelligence that is masked by his sense of humor. He doesn't come across as being as smart as he is, so he's that much more effective."

THE 3 SOUL'S URGE OR DESIRE: CREATIVITY

2nd Desire: W as a Vowel

George W. enjoyed being fun. At Andover, in the spring of his senior year, he played stickball. This was probably the worst squad that the coach ever coached, but George W. made it fun for everyone. One thing his fellow ball players remembered was how he taught the guys to chew Tootsie Rolls and spit the brown juice on the ground so it looked as though they had chewing tobacco in their cheeks, the way the real ball players did. Fun things such as this helped keep up their morale.

The first thing he did in his freshman year was play baseball. In his sophomore year, he became the president of his fraternity, Delta Kappa Epsilon, the same fraternity his dad had joined. George W. couldn't be the best academically so he did what he did best at Andover: became a social leader.

In his senior year he became a cheerleader, and that was really something because most of the fellows who auditioned didn't make it—but George W. was made "head cheerleader." He was a true 3 in that he was very active and full of life and wit, and at the same time he was a true 7 working toward a profession.

His father was the honorary chairman of an organization called PULL (Professionals United for Leadership), an effort to have a mentor and some good role models for minority kids. George W. was one who would work with these children. He met them dressed in torn khakis and took them on trips to prisons to show them the danger of living wasted lives. He played basketball with them. He was at his best helping kids like these. He was also a very popular little league coach at one time in Midland, Texas.

This was certainly true during the stressful first days at the super strict school, Andover. But he never allowed the hardship to get through to him and was a sheer inspiration to his fellow classmates.

A friend said this of George W.: "Before senior year, I thought George was a spontaneous party animal. When you got to know him as just another student at Yale, he did not come across as a serious person, but when you really got to know him, he was."

Behind the 3 Root: Sensitive Leadership

Here we see the influence of the adjective numbers behind the 3. From his biography, I see where all this applies to George W. He had many ambitions and fulfilled them all: went to the same schools as his father, became a pilot and served as an F-102 pilot for the Texas Air National Guard, started his own oil and gas business in Midland in 1975, and got together a group of partners who bought the Texas Rangers baseball franchise in 1989. Then he went into politics. He was elected governor of Texas in 1994 before being elected the President of the United States in 2000. And indeed he is known for having a tactful approach and appreciating it in others. We could see that in his eyes during his great debate with Al Gore for the presidency in 2000 when Gore walked into his space spewing words at him. Though Bush looked surprised, he maintained his dignity.

II. MIND/PERSONALITY

Being dual, the W also affects the Mind/Personality This area includes the way one thinks and the way one dresses. The first Personality number is 8, the business-success look, then 3, freer-flowing styles and more color. Here again, both vibrations are seen in his personality and attire from the time he is a boy, and that makes for a very interesting combination. Lets look first at the 8 Personality.

8 Mind/Personality: An Idea Person
1st Personality: The W as a Consonant

When George W. was just a boy, he greatly admired his father. He followed the same educational path and even attended the same schools (Andover, Yale, and Harvard). When his father began speculating on oil interests, Georgie, as he was called, would go along with him to watch the drilling, and later on he followed his father into politics. George Sr. loved golf and baseball, and Georgie looked forward to mornings on the golf course and playing baseball in school.

There was no significant office to run for at Yale, so there he found his achievements mainly in sports and fraternity life, two things in which his father had also participated.

Appearance

The truth is, George W. was known as a terrible dresser (more of the negative side of the 3) with bad taste in sports shirts, and he wore cowboy boots (probably to make him taller), which he propped up on his desk. He was always seen with a wad of chewing tobacco in his cheek.

3 Mind/Personality: The Cock-eyed Optimist
2nd Personality: The "W" as a Vowel

Here again is a combination of the 8 and 3: the 8 desiring a profession while the 3 makes it fun and sociable—a good combination really.

At school he would offer such witty insights about people walking by that the guys would be crying with laughter. But his remarks also showed intelligence. One of his classmates, Lanny Davis, used to kid him that his big secret was how smart he was and he didn't want anybody to know it.

Appearance

Here is that 3 influence in the clothes he chose to wear. At Harvard, he still snapped his gum in class, as he had in school before, and wore his bomber jacket, a typical 3. But he did graduate in 1975 with a degree in business administration. He made his home in Midland, which was the richest town in America by the early 1980s. There he would wear his cowboy boots. And he certainly was attractive, outgoing, and popular. His little sister Doro said, "We all idolized him. He was always such fun and wild. You always wanted to be with him because he was always so daring."

Behind the 8 Root: Good Health and Spirits

Here we see the influence of the adjective number, 17, behind the 8. In his case, he was in excellent health and spirits, never tired, and never flaunted his money. He was always one of the guys.

III: TOTAL EXPRESSION

The vowels and consonants added together give us the *Total Expression*. This is the same number whether the W is used as a vowel or as a consonant, so here we have one identifying number that tells us more about the whole person and what he or she is best suited for. Some call it *Destiny*.

The 6 Expression: Nurturer/Comforter

Before George W. was married, his little sister Doro was so much younger than he that he was almost a surrogate parent to her, so even at a young age, George W. had great appreciation for his family. He and Laura Welch were engaged five weeks after they met and married three months later. They were so different they complemented each other: he impulsive and energetic, she the quiet lady librarian type. When they wanted a family, Laura had trouble conceiving so they decided to adopt. But as often happens, once they made that decision Laura learned she was pregnant with their twin daughters, Jenna and Barbara.

George W. ran for Ann Richard's office as governor of Texas in 1994 because he was upset with her remark about his father in the

1988 Democratic Convention: "Poor George. He was born with a silver foot in his mouth." George W. was financially comfortable as a salaried employee of his Texas Rangers, but he thought he could run Texas better and he did want to get back into politics.

When he was younger, he was impulsive. If a decision was to be made on anything from where to eat to how to react to a campaign snafu, in moments he'd say, "This is what we've got to do" and he'd be off and out the door before anyone was out of their chair. He was always willing to take on the responsibilities no one else wanted. He always insisted on finishing a project he had started. He made his decision quickly and stuck with it, regardless of consequences. But in 1988, while campaigning for his dad, he finally lost that impetuousness of blurting out an answer as soon as he heard the problem. Now he would hear out the problem and even ask one or two other people to state the problem as they saw it, hear them out, and not interrupt. Now, behaving more like his father, George W. was listening more. He had matured.

Behind the 6 Root: Ambition

From his biography, I see where all this applies to George W. The 15 is interested in the welfare of others and is willing to take on responsibility (the 6 root). As much as they love home, they are willing to travel whenever necessary.

IV: Inner Guidance

Inner Guidance Number 3: Communication and Sociability

George W. doesn't always take his problems seriously for he has an optimistic outlook. He comes up with creative solutions and enjoys discussing them. He is enthusiastic, but he may scatter his energies and may have his worries.

V: Birth Path

Birth Path 6: Humanitarian

Besides their twin daughters, President and Mrs. Bush have their dogs, Spot and Barney, and a cat named India. There is a great amount of love and respect for each other in their family. In fact, George W. never ever heard his parents yell at or criticize each other.

President Bush entered the presidency with initiatives to help the people, first to return to them a nice portion of their tax money to stimulate the economy. Secondly, he wanted to reduce taxes overall for all Americans, but especially those near poverty. His other initiatives are to improve public schools by strengthening local control and insisting on their accountability, saving and strengthening Medicare and Social Security, and giving better pay and better equipment to our military in order to strengthen it the best way possible. In March 2002, he voiced his concern about small businesses and vowed to make things easier for them.

Birth Path 33: Selfless Giving

His Birth Path is 33 when 1946 is added as 10 + 10 (1 + 9; 4 + 6). We have seen this compassion from both President Bush and First Lady Laura since 9/11. They have done their best to comfort and soothe those who lost so much in that tragedy as well as the families of the soldiers who lay wounded or have died to bring peace to Afghanistan.

VI: GOLDEN GOAL

Golden Goal 3: The Retirement Years

There are many talents longing to be expressed. He will find creative outlets through the spoken or written word, so this is the time to write that book. Any creative interest will blossom now, and there is opportunity for a rich, full life, perhaps greater now than ever realized before, if energies are not wasted. This is a good retirement number and there will be chances for pleasant long-distance travel.

VII: KARMIC LESSON

Karmic Lesson 4: Work Must Be Fun

It's true he made all his work fun, not only for himself, but also for the others involved. This was an easy Karmic Lesson for him to learn because a 4 shows up on his chart in the "Opportunities" during his first cycle of life. He learned early from his father to commit baseball cards to memory. This helped him to focus and concentrate, and that's what gave him an edge over the others in pilot school when it came to reading and understanding the plane charts. He also has a 4 in the physical and intuitive Planes of Expression, so he was not missing this lesson entirely.

The lack of 4 is overcome by finding the work you love and, if that's not possible at the time, finding an appreciation for the work of the moment for the purpose it serves. This did indeed happen for George W. He seemed to enjoy all his work immensely because he followed in his father's footsteps just as he wanted to do since he was a little boy. At first he was very impulsive and did things quickly, but he learned to organize efficiently and learned the value of listening to others before making a decision.

VIII: Planes of Expression

Physical 4: The Hard Worker

The missing 4 in his name is made up for here on the physical. A completely missing 4 would not have the stick-to-it-iveness, nor would it be practical and dependable. He was never cocky or "right at all costs," for his father taught him to be respectful of people, and he idolized his father. Until Bible Study and talks with the Rev. Billy Graham, he had a quick temper. After that he was able to control himself.

Mental 3: Imagination

George W. knew how to win people over with humor. When he was running for governor of Texas, his Republican opponent, Jim Reese, knew that George W. as born in Connecticut and tried to use that as a reason he shouldn't be governor of Texas. He said, "George W. has a bright future in politics somewhere, but it's not out here." George W. brought up that remark in his own campaign, saying his one regret was that he wasn't born in Midland, Texas, but at the same time he thought it was more important to stay close to his mother, and she happened to be in New Haven, Cconnecticut at the time.

Indeed he can be interesting to listen to and has evidently never been at a loss for words. However, he never was a bluffer or boastful. He didn't have to be. He cared about people.

To get to know the guys at Yale he would ask questions, and he'd remember not only their names but also details they told him, such as where they liked to vacation best. This was a trait of his father's and he did the same so well that his classmates were very impressed. They took it as a sign that he cared.

Emotional 5: Values Freedom

He was at his best helping someone who was struggling. His friend Charlie Younger said, "He would love to see some underdog with the right cause win. If someone was bashing a minority, he would demand, 'Why do you think that way?' All people had worth to George." Younger also said, "Things where people overcome odds to succeed really tug at his heart."

George W. said that the good thing about politics was the fact that every day was different. "Part is mental and part is the stamina to keep you going," he said. When he campaigned, he was tireless. He'd go to 65 doors a day. If no one was home, he'd leave a handwritten note—just as his father did. He loves meeting people and is persuasive.

It is known that George W. drank a lot in his younger days. At 18 when he went to Yale, he concocted fun, as he did at Andover. He went along with the other guys drinking for fun. But when his father ran for a seat in the Senate, lost, and then showed he was resilient and could bounce back, it impressed George W. greatly. He decided he would do less partying and make something of himself.

Intuitive 4: Analytical

This is so important, for the letters involved in the Planes of Expression explain more of his character. To see more clearly the letters involved, let's add them to his inclusion table by placing them under their numbers. The more there are of one letter, the stronger the traits.

4   Physical letters: EEEW
3   Mental letters: ASH
5   Emotional letters: BKULO
4   Intuitive letters: GGRR

Physical Letters

The physical letters in his name are the E and W, making the energetic and freedom-loving 5 the strongest numerical vibration in his name.

Physical E: The Symbol for Energy

There are more Es than any other letter in his name, so these are outstanding traits. The following story was told about his high energy level. Right on George W.'s 31st birthday in 1977, the granddaddy of Texas politics, George Mahan, retired from his congressional seat where he was since 1934 as the longest serving member. Because George W. had no other commitments, he decided to run for it in 1978, which surprised everyone. With the help of his closest friends and business associates, he won victory in the primaries by 8,000 votes. They say he was completely tireless. During the weeks leading up to the June 3rd runoff, they would book him for an early breakfast and an 8 p.m. coffee and it never daunted him. Unfortunately, he lost the election due to dirty politics and mud-slinging lies that damaged his reputation. He went back to drilling oil with the company he founded, Arbusto (Spanish for *bush*).

Here we also find one negative trait that is well known to have been a part of his past: self-indulgence that could lead to poor health. And that was his early days of drinking. The strong side of the E (energy) helped him to overcome this problem. He also smoked for a short while when he was 18 or 19. His mother got very upset and told him he shouldn't smoke. His dad then said, "Barbara, who are you to tell your son he shouldn't smoke as you so deeply inhale your Newport?" She then noticed that all her children had started smoking. That was when she stopped and never smoked again.

Physical W: The Business Letter

Thanks to the W, he had to try, test, and taste things such as alcohol and, for a while, smoking. He graduated from Air Force Pilot Training on December 2, 1969. Military superiors complimented him. They said he was one young member who got high on flying but never on drugs.

He didn't have to go overseas because of the retirement of the F-102, and he was assigned to the reserves. He rented a bachelor pad in a swinging apartment complex in Houston, played volleyball in the pool, drank beer, and dated. But when his dad was running for a Republican seat in the Senate in 1970, he would never drink or do anything that would reflect badly on his father. He applied to and was accepted at Harvard in the fall of 1975. He still drank but wasn't out of control, and he never did drugs.

Mental Letters

Of the 3 Mental letters, there are two with the 1 root: A and S. The one letter with the root of 8 is the H. Here we see all the traits for durable leadership.

Emotional Letters

Emotional letters are very important for a caring and feeling individual. The 2s, 3s, and 6s are the emotional roots involved. Here we find one each of 5 emotional letters: B and K with the 2 root, U and L with the 3 root, and O with the 6 root.

Emotional K: Inspired

The K letter vibration was also very important in helping him get over a drinking problem in his youth, because it is a letter of light and desires mastery over the lower self. When George W. drank, he never got mean. He was just a social drinker and didn't even suspect he had a problem. Laura noticed that he would have more comeback answers than usual and his voice would get louder. People said that when he drank he was funnier and even more of a smart mouth.

It all came to a head one weekend when he and Laura and a group of his friends got together to celebrate their 40th birthdays. They had a great dinner and shared many bottles of good wine. No one remembered George W. getting drunk, but the next morning he woke up with a severe hangover that robbed him of his energy. He hated that feeling so he just stopped drinking. He told the *New York Times* he quit for life—that he didn't need alcohol anymore and was stronger than it is.

Emotional U: Executive Ability

He graduated from Yale University with a degree in history and from Harvard with a degree in business administration.

Intuitive Letters

George W. has four intuitive letters: two Gs (7 root) and two Rs (9 root). The intuitive letters give a person an inner knowing, an innate wisdom to draw upon, compassion, and a feeling of respect for others.

Intuitive G: Working Alone

This does not mean the G cannot work well with people. The G is a thinker and needs to think things through "alone" before discussions with coworkers. Two 7s in a name gives very strong opinions on politics and religion. At the time of this writing, due to his deep convictions, President Bush plans to take away the right of choice where abortion is concerned. Otherwise he feels individual laws should be left to the states.

IX: CHALLENGES AND OPPORTUNITIES

The Challenges and Opportunities co-exist together for each cycle, so we will look at them together in each time period. President Bush's first cycle is from birth to age 30. During that time, he has the 1 as his first Challenge and the 4 as his first Opportunity. Keep in mind that the challenges are the areas that need to be strengthened and the opportunities are motivating forces that are longing for expression.

1st Cycle: The 1 Challenge and the 4 Opportunity

The 1 Challenge: Overcome Dependence

George W. never really had to prove anything, because he felt unconditional love and support from his family since birth. His parents never placed demands on him, but he knew they expected the best of him, and, whether he realized it or not, his challenge was to live up to their expectations, especially his mother, who demanded high achievement of all her children. He was actually terrified of failure. The adults in his life who knew him best knew he had potential for greatness. And he certainly did test his assertiveness, but never in a way that would embarrass his parents, for he admired them greatly—especially his father, whom he wanted to emulate. The one boyhood challenge was to play ball well, and he was stockily built so they gave him a catcher's mitt. But that was good because, unlike all the other players, he was on the field all the time and he enjoyed that.

The 4 Opportunity: Working for Your Future

When the 4 occurs in the first cycle, it means the child will have a job early in life. This is either due to necessity or the opportunity to lay the foundation for a chosen life's work. Either way, the feeling is clear that there is no time for play but to work to free the self from limitations. In this case it was an opportunity to set the foundation for his life's work.

The 4 is the vibration of the honest achiever. This is the time he would think seriously about setting the foundation for the future, to work towards goals and for security. He would start a savings and look into speculations that pay interest. This is also a family vibration and makes him feel the need to take responsible action for your family's best interest. By the time George W. was 30, he had obtained a degree in history at Yale University and a degree in business administration at Harvard.

2nd Cycle: The 4 Challenge and the 8 Opportunity

The 4 Challenge: Overcome Laziness and Carelessness

George W. had an easy time with this Challenge now because he had it for an Opportunity in the first cycle of his life. It is interesting that it was the one vibration missing in his name (Karmic Lesson) and the fact that he was such a cut-up in school and still managed to be serious enough to do well enough to earn his degrees. He had plenty of help too with this vibration present in the number of physical letters and intuitive letters, so it was not entirely missing in his make-up. It often appeared that he lacked self-discipline because of his eternally optimistic viewpoint and making the best of every negative situation.

At the beginning of his 2nd cycle in 1977, when he was 31, he started the small oil company named Arbusto but didn't start drilling until 1979. He was a "landman," the one who checks maps of land rights at the county clerk's office and then tracks down the owners and makes deals. But he wasn't lucky at choosing drilling sites so he had a difficult time getting started. At the same time, he had the 8 opportunity.

The 8 Opportunity: Material Fulfillment

One material success was the marriage to Laura Welch, just at the beginning of this cycle when George W. was 31. They were engaged five weeks after they met and married three months later.

This really wasn't an easy Pinnacle because the oil was not gushing and they were getting into debt. George W. decided to run for the congressional seat vacated by retiring Texan, George Mahan, and won a victory in the primaries by 8,000 votes. He did work hard toward his goal, campaigning by going door to door to meet people.

In the ensuing campaign he was doing really well until the opponents seriously damaged his standing by bringing up some dirty politics against him from a previous campaign where someone had run an ad in the school paper on his behalf without asking approval. The ad read, "A Bush Bash. Come for free beer and music." That ad was not at all in good taste (pun intended). The opponents discovered it, printed it, and sent the letter to 4,000 members of the Church of Christ.

He lost that campaign because it made him look like he was pushing beer on college students. How true it was to not put his trust in other people. He could have called the paper, as his secretary suggested, and have them print some equally destructive information from his competitor's past having to do with owning a bar but, as the biography states, he preferred to take the high road. He said, "Hance is not a bad person and I'm not going to destroy him in his home-town. This is not an issue. If I try to destroy him to win, I won't win." He just knew from family experience that smear tactics did more damage than good. Indeed he met this with educated intelligence.

3rd Cycle: The 3 Challenge and 3 Opportunity

It is interesting that George W. not only had a 3 challenge and a 3 opportunity at the same time, but the events of his life reflected this exactly in those years.

The 3 Challenge: Overcome Negativity

It was 1985. George W. just turned 39, oil wasn't gushing, and he was in debt, price of oil dropped to $9 a barrel. It hurt, but he refused to lay off his employees. Someone who knew George W. said he never really got depressed, that he never had two bad days in a row. But, he added, "At this time he was walking uphill into a headwind."

When oil prices were at their lowest, he began taking Bible Study classes every Sunday in the church where he and Laura were married and were now attending. One day the teacher asked, "What is a prophet?" "That," said George W., "is when revenues exceed expenditures. No one's seen one out here for a few years."

It was also in this time period when he turned 40 that he decided to stop his social drinking completely. He did not want to do anything to embarrass his father in any way. He respected him too much. He made the best of what could have been a bad situation. He just said, "I don't need it in my life anymore and I'm stronger than it is." And he told the *New York Times*, "I quit for the rest of my life." Near the end of this time period was when President Bush Sr. was running for re-election to his second term, but was defeated by Bill Clinton.

George W. campaigned very hard for his dad but found it an impossible task because of the damaging tactics Ross Perot used because he did not agree with Bush. In the waning days of the campaign, George W. strove to be the ego his father lacked and give the energy his father needed. Even knowing what he did, George W. refused to blast Perot at the state convention. It was not in his belief system to ever smear an opponent, no matter how brutal their attack. It was painful for him to see his father's defeat, but he came to realize that, although his dad excelled at baseball, academics, and oil, it was he himself who was the better politician.

An opportunity presented itself for George W. to sell the company to a group who bought up all the oil companies that were close to being bankrupt, and the buyer would even keep a few of the employees. This was an answer to one problem, but he was concerned for his employees who were suddenly jobless and actually took the time to make a few phone calls and find jobs for them.

It was also during this time period that his father was vice president to Ronald Reagan and about to embark on his own campaign for the presidency. George W. had helped campaign for him before and, as much as he hated to leave Midland, there was nothing to keep him there now. Besides, he enjoyed campaigning and he felt he could use his skills to their best advantage. So he seized the opportunity to move his family to Washington, D.C. and work as an aide in his father's campaign. Once in Washington, George W. found that being there "charged him up." George W. learned at last how to channel his energy, and in this work he discovered his own political skills. His father noticed this and gained a new respect for his son and even turned to him for advice.

Once his father was in office, George W. went back to Texas to prepare himself to run for governor, and then another opportunity presented itself. His long-time business partner called to tell him the Texas Rangers were up for sale and suggested it would give him a great stance from which he could run for governor. So late in 1989 his own investors bought the Texas Rangers, and his mom, wearing a Ranger's jacket, threw the first pitch.

4th Cycle: The 5 Challenge and the 9 Opportunity

The 4th cycle is considered the main cycle that is with us all through life but most prominent during the 4th cycle and from then on. It is amazing that 5 and 9 are this man's number vibrations at this time. If this doesn't make a believer of you, nothing will.

The 5 Challenge: Overcome Impulsive Actions

This cycle began for George W. in 1994 when he turned 48 years old. Think well before acting is what George W. did when he ran for governor of the state of Texas against popular incumbent, Ann Richards, in 1994. His challenge was to show up her weaknesses rather than put more focus on her strengths—and to do it without smearing her in any way. He won by promoting himself as a candidate with the business experience he had in Major League Baseball and character-building education in the oil industry so people would see that he was able to give strong, independent leadership as a governor. He had an agenda that addressed the main issues and concerns of the state. He won the election on November 8, 1994, with 53.5 percent of the vote. He became the first Texas governor to be elected to a consecutive four-year term, winning 68.6 percent of the vote on November 3, 1998.

Just as this 4th cycle started its 10th year, George W. won the presidency. Here is when his most difficult challenges began: with the terrorists' destruction of the World Trade Center on 9/11/01. He was in Florida at the time, just ready to speak to children at a school when he got the word. He would now have to use his freedom wisely and take the right action because he would be responsible for his decisions. His natural urge would be just as ours: to want to strike back immediately. But he did what he learned was best to do—that is, to not act on impulse, but to consider all angles and plan wisely. He definitely will have this challenge for quite awhile: to think before acting.

The 9 Opportunity: Completions and Compassion

If ever we need a high vibration equipped with understanding, tolerance, and compassion, it is in the time of war. How fortunate for our president to have this 9-vibrational opportunity at this time. How true that emotions are high and many disappointments must be faced. But he does love people, has compassion, and finds joy in lifting up their spirits whenever and however possible. He proved that when he went immediately to Ground Zero and put his arms around the firefighters and spoke with the grief-stricken people. He proved it when he sent food to Afghanistan at the same time he sent our military to free them from a terrorist stronghold. He feels their pain and he feels their joy. He is deep inside this beautiful humanitarian vibration at a time he needs it most to keep his courage.

A 9 cycle is not a good time to start something new, because it is a cycle that completes projects from before. And President George W. knows the war won't be finished in a year or two, yet he felt had no other alternative.

The 9 cycle makes you want to donate time and money to worthwhile projects charities, and the last I read was that our president is donating a lot of his personal money to aid the victims of the 9/11 tragedy.

In conclusion, I am happy I decided to use George W. Bush as an example for a chart. I feel it is not only timely, but also so very revealing on his inner nature according to his biography. At the same time I learned something valuable, too: that W not only means the "double-you," but the energies of the double vibrations don't stop and start at certain points. They are always with you. One may be more prominent than the other at certain times, but they co-exist, giving the person multifaceted character.

Florence Campbell, early numerologist, wrote that W is the most difficult of all letters, that it is a strong force for good or ill, depending on the character of the person who owns it, and that it is an explosive force in a lesser soul and a great power in a great one. May the strength and the power of the positive W be the force that remains with our president during these trying times.

Part Two:

Your Journey Continues

Your Address

The root number of your address tells you what to expect life to be like in that dwelling. If you are in an apartment, the overall feeling is the street address, and the apartment number is your personal rooms. Let me give a few examples. My parents lived for years in a home where the root was a 5, a number of activity, change, people, and friends, as well as travel and new experiences. There was never a dull moment. They loved people, and friends were drawn to them to visit quite often. There was a lot of activity: good conversation, card games, barbecues, luncheons, and dinners. Friends came from a distance and would stay overnight or for a week. After Dad retired, he and Mother would travel in a motor home for a good part of the year. It was a typical 5, and they loved it. When Dad died, we moved Mother close to us to a retirement center of apartments in nice ranch style houses. Her apartment number is 7. This is a complete change from all the activity she knew. Seven is quiet and reserved. She rarely has company anymore. It is very quiet and no activities except at the main center a block away.

When I did the research for my first book, *The Secret Science Behind Numerology*, we lived in a house that came to a 7. The vibrational feeling there was incredible for me at the time, because a 7 is so conducive to research, analysis, and writing. I had the quiet, peaceful feeling I needed for what I wanted to do. I have noticed through the years that each address we had reflected the activity and feeling of where we lived.

To find the vibration of your address, do the following:

House

Simply add the numbers in the address down to the root. For example, 56783 = 29/**11** (11 is the root; *The 2 and 9 are the adjectives that describe the root).* Remember: 11 is a Master Number not reduced to its root of 2.

Apartment

The apartment numbers are what affect you personally; the street address of the apartment gives you a clue to the environment and conditions around you.

Some apartment numbers include a letter, such as 202-C. Then the number of the letter expresses what you desire there. In this case, the root is 4, a number of work, order, and the predictable, whereas the C is 3, a desire for more fun and variety. That was the case for my mother being in a number 7C. The 7 is so quiet and reserved and the C (3) is her desire for more company, fun, and variety.

Street number

For streets such as 27th Street, you will add this to your personal address to find the vibration of your neighborhood. Realize that for you personally, your house or apartment number by itself has the strongest influence. Following is a chart of what to expect at the root number of different addresses.

1 ADDRESS

This is a wonderful house for people with individual tastes and creative ideas. This vibration will give you opportunities to take the lead in your work or community, if that is your desire. Here you will feel a self-confidence to help you attain your individual pursuits for success. You can live alone here and be comfortable. If you have a partner, you may both want to have the say-so, so be aware of the fact that the 1 home encourages independence.

2 ADDRESS

In this home you will want companionship and activities that involve your family and/or friends. It is a wonderful home for love and sharing, but uncomfortable to be alone. You will be most happy if you have a place for everything and everything in its place. You and your companion will enjoy quiet and peaceful surroundings, but if you have been used to and like loud parties, you will feel uncomfortable here, for this is a vibration for well-mannered, refined people.

3 ADDRESS

This is a great house to entertain in, for it has a cheerful, friendly feeling and many laughs and fun. It is a good place, too, for the writer or anyone who has an artistic sense. It is also a very comfortable house and people will enjoy visiting. Romance can bloom here and as easily end if it isn't one of trust. You will want to splurge on things that may affect your finances, so you must be careful not to buy on impulse. These homes are very pretty or pretty messy. The 3 scatters energies and hates to have to keep things in order.

4 ADDRESS

This is a great home for children to have the discipline of learning to play a musical instrument or other activity that requires special training. Although this vibration insists on saving for financial security, it also inspires fun-loving family togetherness. You will want to keep things neat and orderly. Good business opportunities avail themselves. It is a pleasure to work in the garden or organize and plan for the future. You'll be happiest if you feel well-respected in your community.

5 ADDRESS

If you like variety, adventure, activities, and travel, this is a great place to live. Nothing stays the same for long in a 5 vibration. It demands constant change, new experiences, and the unexpected. This is not the place to be if you want a quiet, orderly life. Your phone will ring off the hook; people will want to come to visit or may just drop in unexpectedly. You may be called out of town on business or may decide to take trips quite often. You will be tempted to try, test, and taste all life has to offer.

6 ADDRESS

If you are looking for a really cozy place to come home to, this is it. It's perfect for a family with children and close relatives. This is a comfortable and nurturing place to be, and you'll look forward to evenings after work and on weekends. You won't mind responsibilities living in this haven of good will. The 6 vibration encourages artistic pursuits, gardening, pets, comfort, rest, and all good things families desire. It is a wonderful place to retire after the children are on their own.

7 ADDRESS

If you crave time alone to study, enjoy nature, meditate, or write a book, this is a great place to be. If you live alone and like it, this is perfect. If you have a loving partner, you will both enjoy your moments of aloneness together or apart. A family with children will find that the children will either want to be home to play or study quietly in their rooms, or they will feel the need to go somewhere else to play. The 7 vibration instills the feeling of independence and wanting to learn more about things of interest, especially in the spiritual or scientific world. Ministers love the metaphysical ambiance of this comfortable and quiet home. You wont have a lot of company here unless you invite them.

8 ADDRESS

If you want to have your business at home, this is the ideal place for it. There isn't the domestic feeling here that you would have in the 6 home. Thoughts will be on executive undertakings, organizing, and leading the way for greater financial reward. This home is more showy than comfortable. Usually the company you have here are those with whom you have business dealings. Here you can gain that position of power as long as you organize everything and keep your focus on your goal. You definitely need to take out time for rest and vacation.

9 ADDRESS

This is a wonderful home for those who are free of intolerance and judgment. The 9 is a humanitarian vibration that embraces all people of all types with a feeling of brotherly love. Your feelings of joy are greatly heightened here, and negative feelings seem stronger too, for the 9 is quite emotional. It loves stronger, cries harder, laughs easier, and feels deeper than any other. This is a great place for the aspiring artist or actor. The love for drama and art are very evident in this unique home. The artist will create the greatest works and the actor will be able to portray the deepest levels of emotion. Anyone else will inherit an artistic sense in decorating this home. Passion, love, and romance can be at their height. Disappointments can be equally as devastating. In this home, there will be many emotional experiences. When the inhabitant has learned the joy of giving from the heart, this is a happy home indeed.

Numbers are a part of our everyday life: Our address, phone number, social security number, place of work, the way to find friends, businesses, evaluate scores, tell time, tune in to the radio, to television, the Internet, everything. The moment of your birth has its hour and minute and so do all the special events in your life. When you understand that numbers represent rates of vibration, and each one has its own characteristics, traits, and qualities, and you learn what they are, a whole new world of knowledge opens up to you. It is a journey that never ends, and having this knowledge makes life logical and interesting.

QUICK STUDY OPTIONS

The following information is something you can use as a quick study. For this you do not have to make a chart; just remember the meanings of the numbers and letters. Enough information from this alone will amaze your friends.

- ✧ **Birth day:** You at maturity. See Birth Day Chart (pg. 83).
- ✧ **Number of letters in your Birth Name:** Your special raits and peculiarities. See Chart 1 (pg. 114).
- ✧ **Your first name** is about you personally. Analyze same as whole name.
- ✧ **The first letter (Cornerstone):** The key to reveal your natural approach and initial reactions to life's experiences.
- ✧ **The first vowel:** Your spiritual outlook and inner motivation.

❖ **The middle letter (Keystone):** A pivot point that helps carry out the initial action of the first letter.

❖ **The last letter (Capstone):** The destination or aim to be accomplished.

❖ **Your middle name:** Your secret self, unless you use it instead of your first name.

❖ **Your last name:** Your inherited tendencies.

There is no end to the journey. The more you learn, the more there is yet to learn. I went from studying names to analyzing words. I discovered that words, analyzed like a name, describe themselves perfectly. Once you understand number vibration and its many aspects, you may want to study astrology, tarot, and the Cabalah. Numbers are the foundation for all of them. In fact, you can compare the numbers on your chart with the same numbered tarot card and find agreement and learn even more. The 12 houses in astrology are numbered and also agree. So no matter which you decide to study, the meanings of numbers remain the same. Numbers are the basis of all sciences, physical or metaphysical.

I loved this study because it made me realize why we all think so differently. We are not all alike. That makes us quite interesting. I know you can study your personal day, month, and year, and so many other things. But what we have covered here are the nuggets of knowledge, the keys that you will find most helpful. To know the treasures locked in your name is knowledge most wonderful and revealing. It is one sure way to understand our family better and ourselves. To know the vibrational aura where we live is also helpful when it comes to choosing our next home. Other than these, it is not wise to let anyone or anything else rule our lives.

To be explicit, I once did a chart for someone that included his personal days for two years of his life and he became so dependent on it he couldn't function without consulting those daily numbers. This is not necessary. The last chapters will give you something much more substantial to use, where you don't have to become dependent on anything outside of yourself. There is a powerful natural law that is so prevalent around us, but very few have noticed it.

The Vibratory Significance of 9/11

If you've been on the Internet, you probably remember this e-mail that floated around at the time:

- ✧ The date of the attack : 9/11. 9+1+1= 11.
- ✧ September 11th is the 254th day of the year: 2 + 5 + 4 = 11.
- ✧ After September 11th there are 111 days left until the end of the year.
- ✧ Twin Towers: Standing side by side, look like the number 11.
- ✧ The first plane to hit the towers was Flight 11.
- ✧ New York: The 11th state added to the Union.
- ✧ New York City: 11 letters.
- ✧ Afghanistan: 11 letters.
- ✧ The Pentagon: 11 letters.
- ✧ Ramzi Yousef (convicted of orchestrating the attack on the WTC in 1993): 11 letters.
- ✧ Flight 11: 92 on board: 9 + 2 = 11.
- ✧ Flight 77: 65 on board: 6 + 5 = 11.
- ✧ Emergency number is 911: 9 + 1 + 1 = 11.
- ✧ Osama bin Laden adds up to 110, the number of floors in the WTC towers.

❖ "Payback Time" has 11 letters, and so does "World War III."

Whenever a world-stirring event takes place, people become number-conscious and want to know the meanings of the date of the happening. In recent times, 9/11 is probably the most talked-about number, and newspapers struggled to find answers to the meanings of them. I invariably get calls from journalists at times such as these, who are eager to shed some light on a situation where numbers are involved.

The numbers involved *are* significant, for every number represents a rate of vibration, and each vibration creates a different form with its own positive and negative polarities. In others words, every number in its positive aspect is overwhelmingly good. In its negative aspect the clouds form and the results are either unconstructive or destructive. When we look at a terrifying situation, we naturally see the destructive side of the vibration. Both 9 and 11 are vibrational rates great enough to extend over the world.

Ordinarily, 9 is the humanitarian vibration. It is compassionate because it understands people and exudes an aura of love. People sense this about those with the 9. You might say the 9 loves everyone and everyone loves the 9. But the negative 9 is very immature, disrespects other people, keeps the focus on selfish gain, and thinks its wrongdoings are justified.

When it comes to the Master Number 11, we have another powerful vibration. It can be very, very good, or it can be simply horrid. Elevens are leaders, good or bad. If I had to choose a number for the happening that would start World War III, it would be an 11 for the following reasons:

❖ The 11 has a feeling of power, but with an undertone of nervous tension.

❖ Eleven is the Birth Path of many fine ministers, but also of religious fanatics. The enemy brings their religion into it to make themselves believe they are fighting a holy war.

❖ Some well-known political leaders have this name number or Birth Path: Adolf Hitler, Osama bin Laden, and Saddam Hussein giving all three an inner guidance number of 22—a super sneak, extremely crafty.

The negative side of this vibration is that of utter frustration for expecting too high a standard of others and no one being able to live up to their expectations.

The destructive side will use their power for their own selfish reasons and can be incredibly cruel.

The 11 is significant because it represents duality. The root of 11 is 2. Two is composed of two 1s that are diametrically opposed. People the world over are very quickly becoming one of two types, and it has nothing to do with races and religions. It is instead those who are aware of a higher power and seek peaceful co-existence, and those who have uncontrolled rage inside them, bent on destroying anything and everything. This is the human duality: The two groups, the aware and the unaware, the sane and the insane. These two types of people cannot get along together.

COINCIDENCE OR TWIST OF FATE?

There is a debate going on today whether or not we create our world by influences around us. Headlines in several papers have been: "Mounting evidence links TV viewing to violence" (Christian Science Monitor) and "TV viewing linked to adult violence" (Associated Press). Research groups have concluded it does. Of course this includes violent movies. There have been more than 1,000 studies in the past 30 years, and scientists and psychiatrists now say that the correlation between the two is no longer debatable—that it is an established fact.

Then there are those like Jonathan Freedman, a professor at the University of Toronto, and many members of the broadcasting industry who do not believe in the statistics of proof. The problem for people such as this is that there is no *known* universal law that gives the ultimate proof of "established facts." But there IS a relatively unknown universal law that does prove it: the law of magnetic attraction. This is explained in more detail in the next chapter, but here I would like to point out some amazing coincidences. Or are they twists of fate? You decide.

Four years before 9/11, Nicole Kidman and George Clooney made a movie called *The Peacemaker* (1997). Watching it was like seeing everything that led up to and almost including 9/11.

Here we have all the elements: *nuclear explosives* (jet fuel), a *plane* taking the *terrorist* to *New York City,* the *Twin Towers* clearly visible, the intent to *destroy New York.*

Before this movie, there was Irwin Allen's *The Towering Inferno,* one in a string of disaster movies of the 1970s. This one was promoted as a tribute to *firefighters and their heroic work:* "The Towering Inferno"(1974) is not just about the world's *tallest building in flames,* it's the story of people.... Of heroism, of evil, of love, of drama," said the ads. "It is about the tallest building in the world being on fire; there's no way down there's no way out."

I recently saw one of the posters for this movie, and it was like seeing the 9/11 towers in flames again. In fact, the flames were coming from about the same area of the first tower of the World Trade Center. Posters were made of this fiery scraper for Australia, Denmark, Germany, Belgium, Finland, France, Italy, Japan, Mexico, Poland, Romania, South Africa, Spain, and the United Kingdom (Ireland, Scotland, England). Now, you tell me, if there is a law of magnetic attraction and our thoughts are magnetic energies, and you have millions of people viewing something like this the world over, feeling the emotion of it, and then later buying the videos to view over and over again making that magnetic field all the larger and more powerful, is it not possible they have begun the creation of a monster?

Several movies were being filmed, just months before the disaster, that vividly displayed the twin towers: *Zoolander, Serendipity,* and the Al Pacino film *People I Know.* No destruction of the towers, but the focus is there. After 9/11 all three films removed the towers in editing so as not to traumatize movie-goers.

Then there was *Time Machine* that edited out moon rocks raining on Manhattan (ame location) and there was *Spiderman* climbing up one of the World Trade Center towers. That storyline was scrapped as well.

There was the movie, *Big Trouble,* that was supposed to open in September 2001. After 9/11 it was pulled from its release date because the climax of the movie involved two terrorists sneaking a gun, nuclear bomb, and two hostages past through airport security in Miami. That was supposed to be funny. It's interesting what affects some people as humor.

Actor Jackie Chan had to rewrite his movie project entitled *Nose-bleed* because the plot was too coincidental to 9/11. He was to star as a window-washer on *the World Trade Center* who puts up a fight against *terrorists* hell-bent on blowing up the Statue of Liberty.

A hip-hop group released an album depicting an exploding World Trade Center on the cover, a cover they designed months before 9/11. And several movies and TV shows were made before 9/11 that showed destruction of the twin towers.

This must have been the mindset of many creative people at the same time. This is called *mass consciousness*, and its influence tends to grow. All that negative energy of the vibratory rate of 11 converged on the 11th.

What the screenwriters do not understand is the law of attraction that they in their ignorance are asking for destruction by putting their focus on these things. Just imagine the good they could do by writing the right scripts.

You all have heard the story of "The Hundredth Monkey," where one monkey decides to wash off his food before eating it. At first the other monkeys on the island looked at him funny, but they decided to try it, liked it, and did it from them on. On another island where monkeys were not aware of this new strategy, monkeys there began to wash their food off too. Was it a thought that they tuned into? What about inventions that happen on both sides of the world at the same time? That happens too. Is it possible that we pick up on other people's thoughts? If we do, could we possibly also pick up on or tune into radio waves, TV waves, cell phone waves, and on and on...? Let's examine this further in the next chapter.

The Vibratory Secret of Manifestation

Before ending this book, I would like to share a powerful secret with you: the vibratory secret of manifestation. What I'm about to tell you could greatly improve your chances of being completely in control of your life. First I'll give you the secret, then the scientific background, and then some examples and how to make it work for you. The secret is: When you focus on an idea for any length of time—with emotion—you start to vibrate with it. Then the law of attraction sets in and draws it to you, *unless* you allow negative thoughts to take over, because negative thoughts cancel the positive attraction.

THE SCIENTIFIC BACKGROUND

It cannot be stressed enough that we live in a vibrational universe. Everything from seemingly empty space to solid matter vibrates. The key to the entire universe is found in the wavelength of vibrations. Scientists have actually measured our three-dimensional world as having the wavelength of 7.23 centimeters, so this is not fantasy or imagination. It is fact.

Each wavelength has its own sound, sound causes vibration, *and vibration causes form!* If you put sand crystals on a radio speaker and turn on the sound, those sand crystals will dance around and change patterns with each word and strain of music. These wavelengths are separated the same as the notes on a musical scale.

William Eisen, who was associated with the Jet Propulsion Laboratory in Pasadena, California, and who discovered the English Cabalah, researched the vibrational frequencies of the musical scale and brought to light some very interesting phenomena by translating the numbers of the wavelengths into their letters (one system of Cabalah). Briefly, there are 88 keys on the piano with 12 half tones in each octave. All 12-tone intervals are exactly equal. The frequency of low A, the lowest note of the 88 keys, is 27.50. Note what happens when we put the corresponding letters to those numbers: BGEO. It actually spells out "be geo," of Earth. Geo is a prefix for Earth, as in geology, geography, and so on.

The vibratory frequency eight octaves higher, the A above the last high C on the keyboard, is 7,040.0. Put letters to that 704 and we have the word GOD. Cabalistically, this tells us that frequencies start from here on Earth where we "B GEO" (be Earth) and continue on into infinity to God. (To read all the detail concerning this, see his book, *The Universal Language of Cabalah*.)

Vibrations exist throughout the universe as well as on planet Earth. Through the science of spectroscopy, we can tell what minerals and elements exist on each planet. Each element has its own pattern that never changes, and by use of the spectroscope the light that comes in from the planet is transformed into parallel rays that can be measured by their wavelengths and compared to known elements on earth. As above, so below. (This science behind numerology is explained more thoroughly in my book *The Secret Science of Numerology*.)

We are actually living in many dimensions at once, separated only by wavelength. There is the dimension where the radio waves, TV waves, Internet waves, and thought waves exist unseen to us until we tune them in. Every time we change a radio station, a TV channel, or a Website, we are tuning in to different wavelengths *that remain invisible and nonexistent to us until we tune them in!* We are receptors ourselves and, if our thoughts are on the same vibratory wavelength as on any other of these dimensions, we pick up on it in the form of impressions. Ever remember saying, "Now where did *that* thought come from?" Once we realize how we tune in to things *out there*, the next step is to realize that we can get what we ask for the same way.

THE LAW OF ATTRACTION

On August 8, 2000, a psychologist on the radio said that psychologists have learned that the world gives us what we ask of it. We are in a magnetic field and attract that which vibrates to our thoughts. More people are familiar with the healing areas of the earth in Lourdes, France, and in Sedona, Arizona, two locations with the highest of magnetic fields for healing. But few know that we create magnetic fields with our thoughts.

A group projecting the same thought is very powerful. An experiment was performed in Washington, D.C. in 1993. A group meditated on peace, and crime went down. The politicians knew about it and saw the results. This was never reported in major news. It was written in scientific literature.

Again, the law is that when you focus on an idea for any length of time, with emotion, you begin to vibrate at that frequency. Then the law of attraction sets in and all things of that vibratory nature come to you. It is given us in Bible verse Mark 11:24: *"So I tell you, whatever you ask for in prayer, believe that you have received it, and it will be yours."* And the word *prayer* vibrates to 11, so prayer can nullify the vibrations of negative 11s.

Famed opera singer Enrico Caruso proved this attraction/vibration connection. When he was at a dinner party, he would tap his crystal goblet to hear its note. Then he would sing that note louder and louder until the goblet started to vibrate and then would burst. Nothing else in the room was touched, just the goblet that was of the same vibrational tone. Scientists have played with the tuning fork and found that when it rings loudly, some objects will vibrate with it, whereas others remain untouched and all for the same reason: They are of the same rate of vibration.

Haven't you noticed that when you focus on some idea, all of a sudden many other thoughts on that subject come to you? That is the law of attraction in action. The actual manifestation takes a little longer. The way the law works is that it gives us more of the vibration we emit, so it is imperative we make positive thinking a habit, for once you allow negative thoughts to take over, they will cancel the positive attraction. Remember that we are dealing with the Law of Attraction. What you need to remember is this: *What I think, I feel. What I feel, I vibrate. What I vibrate, I attract.*

That is Law of Attraction that leads to manifestation! Write that down. Memorize it. Once you understand the Law of Attraction, you can consciously create your good, rather than idly hoping it will happen. Otherwise, you attract your strongest vibration by default.

True Examples of the Law at Work

Linda Clark, author of *Get Well Naturally*, was determined to find a cure for cancer, but when she put her focus on the disease she began to vibrate with it to the extent that she attracted it herself and it was the cause of her death.

On the other hand, Norman Cousins is famous for having overcome a degenerative spinal disease by ignoring it, and he did so by turning his focus on funny movies and laughing himself to health. The incurable disease disappeared and he lived many more years in good health. Do you see how their thoughts determined the health of their organs and how the focus of their attention became their reality? If you find yourself gritting your teeth or furrowing your brow, you are attracting negativity. Your thoughts are directly connected to your respiration and signals are sent through your body to be on alert. This causes dis-ease.

Those two examples have to do with health. It is the same for money. A well-known story is that of actor Jim Carrey. He wanted to be an actor, earning great sums of money. He dreamed about it over and over; he even wrote himself a check for a million dollars to make it seem like it really happened. And we all know from his many successful movies, it did!

I stumbled on this in my life many years ago—but didn't know until recently WHY it worked. But I had a method I followed whenever I really wanted to manifest a desire: I made a list! The first one I can remember making was for attracting the perfect mate. I had a long list of qualities I wanted in a man. My mother was discouraged. She told me I'd never find all those wonderful traits in one man, but it wasn't long after that I met the man of my dreams, and Jeff had every single quality on my list. I told our daughters about this strategy of making a list and focusing on it, and both have since married wonderful men. Both have told me how that advice worked for them, and both know they have the man of their dreams.

I used this strategy of making a list in order to find the right house for us, too. Once we decided to make a change, I made out a list of all the things we wanted for our house, and not only did I focus on that list every day, I talked about it to my unseen guides as I drove to and from work and asked them to find it for us.

Our real-estate agent shook her head. It was doubtful to find everything I wanted in our price range *where* I wanted the house to be located. But one day when Jeff was driving around, he had the impulse to turn onto a no-exit street, and it led him to a house with a sale sign in front. When I saw it, I felt like I was home. Our agent was surprised because this house was advertised with three bedrooms, but it had four! The price was right. The neighborhood was right. Everything on my list was there, including a nice-sounding street name.

These are the steps I use that always work:

✧ Make a list.

✧ Focus on it often and feel happy as you visualize it.

✧ Talk about it to God, your unseen guides, or your guardian angel.

✧ Stir up the emotion of an eager anticipation just knowing it's on its way.

Remember: Worry lowers your vibration and stops the good from flowing. From these examples we can see how important it is to make positive thinking a habit. At all times, be aware of the focus of your attention, for once you allow negative thoughts to take over, they will cancel the positive attraction. The way the Law of Attraction works is that it gives us more of the vibration we emit, whether positive or negative.

I use to wonder how God could answer prayers given in so many different languages. Now I realize it's not the words that are important, it is the vibration we emit. So if we do not get what we have asked for, it's possible we have worried we wouldn't, and that negative feeling actually cancelled the positive attraction.

CHANGING THE WORLD

Now let's look at this on a larger scale. We have entered the 21st century with some pretty heavy social problems, and all are due to the lack of spiritual knowledge, specifically not understanding vibratory attraction. We have children committing crimes. They are taught how by the movies they see and the games they play, movies because of the visual impact and games because of the learned muscle reaction, but materialistic adults can't see the connection! For example, what a parent tells a child becomes a thought that can make or break that child's life. And the games children play are powerful unseen forces that ready a child for action. Too many video games affect a child psychologically.

Scientific studies have proven that those who just close their eyes and see themselves doing something they've never done before are able to do it much easier than those who never even thought about it.

Why? Because when we see ourselves doing something, our muscles respond to our thought, and they actually tone up for the job when it is time. Seeing someone doing something such as dancing—or hurting someone—makes it easier for us to do it. The eye/brain connection is extremely powerful. For example, in 1999, four girls in Los Angeles wanted to compete in synchronized swimming championships. All city pools were closed for the winter, so they had to practice without water. By setting their focus on their goal and seeing themselves performing, their muscles responded as though they had trained in a pool, *and they won four gold medals!*

When it comes to children, what is their focus? Violent computer games? Violent movies? Where are the role models for good behavior? *What messages are we giving them through our entertainment media?* What do they have to draw from in our society, unless they are blessed enough to have parents who teach them spiritual values?

I've always been concerned about children and how impressionable they are. I remember how movies affected me when I was growing up, so no one can tell me they don't influence a child. Years ago, when it became possible to rent movies to watch at home, I felt a tinge of horror race through me. Imagine children being able to see movies with evil content and being able to run back to review and study every unthinkable act of violence, or manner of burglary. What does that do to the uneducated mind? The spirit-deprived mind? Well, results have been confirmed:

- ✧ Prisoners who watch these acts of violence over and over are released from prison only to act out what they have seen.

- ✧ Great bank heists have been learned from films and acted out successfully in both Great Britain and the United States—copied exactly as shown in movies.

- ✧ An ABC network study found that 34 percent of young people imprisoned for violent crimes said they had consciously imitated crime techniques that they learned from watching television programs!

- ✧ Twenty two percent of *juvenile* crime is also due to what children have learned from television and movies.

- ✧ More than 1,000 studies confirm that watching violence increases aggressive behavior in children.

✧ According to a study published in the March 2003 issue of the journal *Developmental Psychology,* outcomes such as criminal convictions and spouse abuse by persons in their 20s have been linked with viewing violence on TV at ages 6 to 9.

There is so much violence on television now that it is affecting more and more children. In some the evil influence remains latent in them until they are adults, and then they are prone to be violent. Jeffrey G. Johnson of Columbia University and the New York State Psychiatric Institute had researchers study families in two upstate New York counties. The evidence is overwhelming that aggression is linked to television-viewing. The rate of violence—including assaults, fights and robberies—increases dramatically if teens watch more than three hours a day, and even the cartoons are violent! This study was published in a March 2002 issue of the journal *Science.*

The most recent horror is the hideous, unbelievable violence shown so graphically on one TV show that it influenced two boys to butcher their mother. It seems to me that the guilty ones here are the writers, producers of that show, and the actors willing to partici-pate, plus the ones who sponsor them with their commercials. If it were not for their dangerous influence, this would not have hap-pened. They are as responsible for that woman's tragic death, as her sons that were influenced by their so-called "entertainment."

If you still don't believe we reap what we sow, consider this:

✧ We are overpopulated, and our movie industry promotes sex.

✧ We have gang violence on our streets, and our movie industry promotes violence.

✧ We have a growing disrespect for common decency, and our movie industry promotes this by glamorizing pro-miscuity, drug users, vulgarity, and stupid behavior.

✧ We have young people driving carelessly, causing accidents, and killing themselves, and our movies and TV commer-cials for cars are making dangerous driving habits look "cool."

We all see this, but no one complains. Why? All this proof, and still we hear the materialistic people denying their influence. How often have you heard, "Oh, I saw those movies, or played those games when I was a child and it never affected me!" What they don't realize is that they never clung to those bad images and made them a part of their lives as some children do. Not everyone can throw them off so easily.

In numerology, we learn the 9 basic vibrations. The 2 is the most sensitive and a natural follower; the 1, 7 and 8 are the deepest thinkers with leadership capabilities; and the 9 and 11 are the most impressionable. These can be found in the Birth Path or in the Birth Name. These are the children most vulnerable, though it affects all children in some way. Remember: Everything we see is impressed on living brain cells that stay with us through life, and we draw on these for our actions and reactions. Scary, huh?

Imagine all the training our children get by simply watching violent movies. And we wonder why some of them kill. We see the evidence of this power at work! We must teach our children to be selective in what they choose to see and think about. They must be told that by choosing their thoughts, they create their reality—their life!

What should kids do? Teach them to daydream about things they love, never ever watch movies that are violent, but keep their mind on happy things because you want them to be happy and safe. Let them know that they attract the object of their focus. If they watch graphic violence a lot, that is the emotional food they are eating, and that is what they will have to draw on as reactions in their life. What's worse, they will attract violence because our bodies each have a magnetic field that attracts what it vibrates. Where our thoughts are and what we feel constitute our magnetic body.

We can all tell when we are creating a negative magnetic field, because we will feel just awful. Our feelings are a true barometer for us, a sort of inner guidance system that alerts us when we have begun to attract something disagreeable by giving us a negative feeling. We are dealing with the law of attraction. What we think, we feel. What we feel, we vibrate. What we vibrate, we attract. This is true in health, relationships, career, finances—anything you can think of. It is where we place our focus that is important!

Shakespeare was right: The world is a stage, and we are but players on it. Only most of us are not actors, but re-actors. We react to other people. If someone shouts at us, we shout back at them. We get caught up in their vibration and react from their frequency. We can't always choose how we feel, but we can choose what to do about it. Once we realize this, we can deliberately write our own script and work hard to make it a habit to consciously maintain our own more serene frequency and give a soft unemotional response. Once we accomplish that,miracles begin to happen. We see their attitude soften, and you sense that they look at you differently with a new respect. You have momentarily lessened their negativity and your whole world is lighter and happier. Very few movies teach proper reaction to negative circumstances, and our children need to learn it somewhere.

One excellent movie is titled *The Staircase.* It is a true story about a Christlike man who appears at a time of need to build a special staircase (that goes from the first floor to the choir loft) in a church in a limited area. In the story, he faced negative people who in today's movies would have reason for great violence, one being a gunman pointing a gun right at him, but he handled that and other tense situations with spiritual maturity. After the staircase was built, he disappeared completely, and to this day no one can figure out how he built it. It spirals upward with no signs of any support. Oh, for a man like him to be used as a hero for young people to emulate. They need this kind of influence so much. It could change the world.

Remember what we said in the last chapter about *mass consciousness?* If enough people turn their focus toward peace, anything bad in the works can be averted. We would have to live, breathe, and see peace. Imagine the wonderful things that can happen if the majority of movies would focus on mature, levelheaded responses to situations instead of violence. It could change our world for the better, for you would have millions of people putting their focus on peaceful solutions. Mass mind is a powerful thing. Let's use it for a happy world.

There is a saying, "Life is a work of art designed by the one who lives it." We can design our personal lives by choice when we first understand ourselves by charting our name as we have done in the first part of this book. Then by understanding and using our personal magnetic power, we can manifest good in our own life and for the world.

Now tell me, what is the secret Law of Manifestation?

The Law of Attraction.

How does it work?

What I think, I feel. What I feel, I vibrate. What I vibrate, I attract.

Practice it to prove it to yourself, and then teach it to the world. This is a joyous journey that never ends.

Bibliography

Campbell, Florence. *Your Days are Numbered.* 4th Edition. New York: Ray Long & Richard R. Smith, Inc., 1945.

Eisen, William. *The Universal Language of Cabalah: The Master Key to the God Consciousness.* Marina del Rey, Calif: DeVorss and Company, 1989.

Jordan, Juno. *The Romance in Your Name.* Marina del Rey, Calif. DeVorss and Company, 1984.

Lawrence,Shirley Blackwell, Msc.D. *The Secret Science of Numerology.* Franklin Lakes, N. J.: New Page Books, , 2001.

———. *Numerology and the English Cabalah.* Van Nuys,Calif: Newcastle Pub., 1993.

Lewis, Robert C. *The Sacred Word and Its Creative Overtones: Relating Religion and Science Through Music.* Oceanside, Calif: Rosicrucian Fellowship, 1986.

Mitchell, Elizabeth. *W: Revenge of the Bush Dynasty.* New York: Hyperion, 2000.

Index

A

address, your, 194-195
adjective numbers behind 7 for
    George W. Bush, 177
adjective numbers, the, 19
apartment vibration, 195
As Above number, 150, 151

B

Birth Day Chart, 83-85
Birth Name, 15, 16
Birth Path
    8, 79
    11, 80-81
    5, 75-76
    4, 74-75
    9, 79-80
    1, 72-73
    7, 78-79
    6, 76-78
    33, 82
    3, 73-74
    22, 81-82
    2, 73
Birth Path, 13, 20-21, 71-72
Bush, George Walker, 175-176

C

Challenges, 24, 131, 132
Challenges and Opportunities, 13, 24-26
child, understanding your, 164

child's Total Expression, a, 164-173
children
    and movies, 210, 212, 213
    and television, 210-211
cipher, 58
consonants
    as Mind that makes up
        Personality, 17-18
    as Secret Self that makes up
        Personality, 17-18
consonants, your, 43
Cosmic Parent, 63, 77

D

Desire and vowels, 12
Destiny, vowels and consonants
    combined as, 18
Double-You Chart, the, 28

E

8
    address, 197
    Challenge, the, 138-139
    children, 170-171
    Golden Goal, 95
    Inner Guidance Number, 90
    on the Planes of Expression, 115-116
    Opportunity, the, 146
    Personality appearance, 52
8 Mind/Personality, 52-53

8 Soul's Urge, 39
8 Total Expression, 66-68
18/9, 9 Total Expression and, 69-70
eighth ray meditation and glory, 90, 110
    as "The Psychic Master," 32
    children, 172-173
    Golden Goal, 96
    Opportunity, the, 148
11/2
    Inner Guidance Number, 91-92
    Mind/Personality, the, 45-46
    Personality appearance, 46
    11/2, negative, 46
emotional letters
    for 3, the, 126
    for 2, the, 125-126
    for 6, the, 127-128
emotional plane of expression, 23, 24
examples of the law of attraction at
    work, 207-209

F

53/8, 8 Total Expression and, 68
5
    address, 196
    Challenge, the, 136
    children, 167-168
    Golden Goal, 95
    Inner Guidance Number, 88-89
    Mind/Personality, 48-49
    on the Planes of Expression, 111-113
    Opportunity, the, 144
    Personality appearance, 48-49
5 Soul's Urge, 35-36
5 Total Expression, 61-63
15/6, 6 Total Expression and, 64
fifth ray meditation and severity, 89
first ray meditation and will, 87
4
    address, 196
    Challenge, the, 135-136

children, 166-167
Golden Goal, 94
Inner Guidance Number, 88
Mind/Personality, 47-48
on the Planes of Expression, 110
Opportunity, the, 143
Personality appearance, 48
4 Soul's Urge, 34-35
4 Total Expression, 60-61
48/12/3,
    3 Soul's Urge and, 34
    3 Total Expression and, 60
44/8, 8 Total Expression and, 68
43/7
    7 Soul's Urge and, 39
    7 Total Expression and, 66
14/5, 5 Total Expression and, 62
fourth ray meditation and mercy, 88
Full and Root Numbers of Letters
    Chart, 119

G

Golden Goal, 13, 21-22, 93-94

H

Higher Self vibration, 86
house vibration, 195

I

Inclusion Table, the, 21-22
Inner Guidance Number, 10, 13, 19-20, 86
intuitive letters
    for 9, the, 129-130
    for 7, the, 128-129
intuitive plane of expression, 23, 24

K

Karmic Lesson
    for 3, 41-42

minus-8, 104-105
minus-5, 102
minus-4, 101
minus-9, 105-106
minus-1, 98-99
minus-7, 103-104
minus-6, 102-103
minus-3, 100-101
minus-2, 99-100
minus-0, 106
Karmic Lessons, 13, 22, 97-98
Kundalini and Master Number 33, 155

L

Law of Attraction, th, 206-209, 213
   and manifestation, 207
   at work, examples of, 207-209
Law of Manifestation, 213
Letters on the Planes of Expression,
   119-130

M

Main Challenge, 132
Main Opportunity as top Pinnacle, 140
manifestation, law of attraction and, 207
Master Architect, the, 149, 153
   vibration, 81
Master Number
   88, the, 158
   11, the, 57, 151-153, 201
   55, the, 157
   44, the, 155-156
   99, the, 158
   77, the, 157-158
   66, the, 157
   33, the, 50, 154-155
   22, the, 153-154
Master Numbers, 17, 150-151
   the remaining, 156-158

mental letters
   for 8, the, 124
   for 1, the, 123
mental plane of expression, 23
Mind and consonants, 12
minus-1 children, 99
minus-2
   children, 100
   remedy, 99-100
   weakness, 99
minus-3
   children, 101
   remedy, 100
   weakness, 100
minus-4
   children, 101
   remedy, 101
   weakness, 101
minus-5
   children, 102
   remedy, 102
   weakness, 102
minus-6
   children, 103
   remedy, 103
   weakness, 102
minus-7
   children, 104
   remedy, 104
   weakness, 103
minus-8
   children, 105
   remedy, 104-105
   weakness, 104
minus-9
   children, 106
   remedy, 105-106
   weakness, 105

N

negative 8, 52, 67
negative 11, 58
negative 11/2, 46
negative 5, 49, 62
negative 44, 53
negative 4, 48, 60
negative 9, 54, 69
negative 1, 44, 56
negative 7, 51, 65
negative 6, 50, 63
negative 3, 47, 59
negative 20, 58
negative 22, 61
negative 2, 45, 57
negative traits of
    Master 11, 152-153
    Master 44, 156
    Master 33, 155
    Master 22, 154
9
    address, 197-198
    Challenge, the, 139
    children, 171-172
    Golden Goal, 95-96
    Inner Guidance Number, 90-91
    Mind/Personality, 53-54
    on the Planes of Expression, 116-117
    Opportunity, the, 147
    Personality appearance, 54
    Soul's Urge, 40-41
9 Total Expression, 68-70
19
    as love vibration, 56
    as Testing Number, 56
9-year cycles, the, 131
ninth ray meditation and foundation, 91
Number intensities, 26

Numbers on the Planes of Expression, 107-118
Numerology Chart, Sample, 27
numerology, the roots of, 10-11

O

occupations
    of 8 Total Expression, 67
    of 5 Total Expression, 62
    of 4 Total Expression, 60
    of 9 Total Expression, 69
    of 1 Total Expression, 56
    of 7 Total Expression, 65
    of 6 Total Expression, 64
    of 3 Total Expression, 59
    of 2 Total Expression, 57
1
    address, 195
    Challenge, the, 132-133
    children, 164-165
    Golden Goal, 94
    Mind/Personality, 44
    on the Planes of Expression, 107-108
    Opportunity, the, 141
    Personality appearance, 44
    Soul's Urge, 30-31
    Total Expression, 55
Opportunities, 25, 140
    the Challenges and, 13
order of your chart, the, 12-14

P

Personality, 12
    consonants as Mind that
        make up Personality, 17-18
    consonants as Secret Self that
        make up Personality, 17-18
physical letters
    for 5, 122
    for 4, the, 121

physical plane of expression, 22, 23
Pinnacle, Main Opportunity as top, 140
Planes of Expression, 13, 22-24, 107
positive traits
    of Master 11, 152
    of Master 44, 156
    of Master 33, 155
    of Master 22, 154
Positive, Negative, and Destructive
    Aspects of Numbers chart, 14

Q

quick study options, 198-199

R

rate of vibration, 29
remaining Master Numbers, 156-158
roots of numerology, the, 10-11

S

Sample Numerology Chart, 27
science behind numerology, the, 11-12
scientific background of manifesta-
    tion, the, 205-206
second ray mediation and wisdom, 87
selfless giving energy, 82
7
    address, 197
    Challenge, the, 138
    children, 169-170
    Golden Goal, 95
    Inner Guidance Number, 89-90
    Mind/Personality, 51
    on the Planes of Expression, 114-115
    Opportunity, the, 145-146
    Personality appearance, 51
7 Soul's Urge, 38-39
7 Total Expression, 64-66
17/8, 8 Total Expression and, 68

seventh ray meditation and victory, 90
6
    address, 197
    Challenge, the, 137
    children, 168-169
    Golden Goal, 95
    Inner Guidance Number, 89
    Mind/Personality, 49-50
    on the Planes of Expression, 113-114
    Opportunity, the, 144-145
    Personality appearance, 50
6 Soul's Urge, 36-37
6 Total Expression, 63-64
16/7, 7 Total Expression and, 65-66
sixth ray meditation and beauty, 89
So Below number, 153
Soul's Urge, vowels as, 16-17
street number vibration, 195

T

10/1 Inner Guidance Number, 87
Testing Number, 19 as, 56
third ray meditation and under-
    standing, 88
13/4, 4 Total Expression and, 61
30/3, 3 Total Expression and, 59
33 Master Number, 64
33/6, 6 Soul's Urge and, 37
3
    address, 196
    Challenge, the, 134-135
    children, 166
    Golden Goal, 94
    Inner Guidance Number, 87-88
    on the Planes of Expression, 109-110
    Opportunity, the, 142-143
    Personality appearance, 47
3 Mind/Personality, 46-47
3 Soul's Urge, 32-34

3 Total Expression, 58
Total Expression, 55
　　and vowels and consonants, 12
Total Expression, vowels and
　　consonants combined as, 18
25/7, 7 Total Expression and, 66
22/4 Inner Guidance Number, 92
22/4, 4 Total Expression and, 61
21/3,
　　3 Soul's Urge and, 33
　　3 Total Expression and, 59
26/8, 8 Total Expression and, 68
27/9, 9 Total Expression and, 70
23/5,
　　5 Soul's Urge and, 36
　　5 Total Expression and, 62
22
　　children, 173
　　4 Soul's Urge and, 35
　　Golden Goal, 96
　　Opportunity, the, 149
twist of fate, coincidence or, 202-204
2
　　address, 195-196
　　Challenge, the, 133-134
　　children, 165-166
　　Golden Goal, 94
　　Inner Guidance Number, 87
　　Mind/Personality, 44-45
　　on the Planes of Expression, 108-109
　　Opportunity, the, 141-142
　　Personality appearance, 45
　　Soul's Urge, 31-32
　　Total Expression, 56-58

U

understanding your child, 164

V

vibratory secret of manifestation, 205
vibratory significance of 9/11, 200-202
vowels and consonants combined
　　as Destiny, 18
　　as Total Expression, 18
vowels and consonants in the Total
　　Expression, 55
vowels and consonants, Total
　　Expression and, 12
Vowels as Soul's Urge, 16-17
vowels, your, 29-30

W

well-known people with
　　Birth Path 8, 79
　　Birth Path 11, 81
　　Birth Path 5, 76
　　Birth Path 4, 75
　　Birth Path 9, 80
　　Birth Path 1, 72-73
　　Birth Path 7, 78-79
　　Birth Path 6, 77-78
　　Birth Path 33, 82
　　Birth Path 3, 74
　　Birth Path 22, 82
　　Birth Path 2, 73

Z

0 Challenge, the, 139-140
0 on the Planes of Expression, 117-118

About the Author

From the time Dr. Shirley Lawrence was still in her teens, her main interests were in music, religion, philosophy, and, later, quantum physics. In 1957, she took the Science of Mind Course directed by Dr. Jack Ensign Addington in San Diego. She graduated from San Diego State University in 1958 with a B.A. in music as a voice major with studies in piano, cello, drums, conducting, and composing, and with performances in opera, musical comedy, and drama. She did post-graduate studies with Theo Verlyn, a well-known voice teacher in the mid-1960s.

When she completed college in 1958, her father gifted her with Florence Campbell's Book, *Your Days Are Numbered.* Being an avid reader, she read it cover to cover and put it aside. Years later, some unusual experiences led her into the study of numbers. People she never met before began asking her if she knew the meaning of numbers. So she attended a seminar on numbers where she learned how to make her own chart—and then she got hooked.

After five years of research in related fields, her first book, *Behind Numerology,* was born. She followed that with the book *Numerology and The English Cabalah,* which continued where the first book left off in the exciting new field of English Cabalah. Along with the publication of those two books, she gave seminars on numerology at Manly Palmer Hall's Philosophical Research Society in Los Angeles in the late 1980s. New Page Books republished her first book as *The Secret Science of Numerology* in June 2001.

In 1992 she obtained her minister's standing and wrote two theses to earn her doctorate in Metaphysical Science from the University of Metaphysics, where she then became a member of Dr. Paul Leon Master's staff. During this time, she spoke at conventions for the University of Metaphysics and the International Metaphysical Ministry and for local groups. She retired in June 2001 and is now continuing her research and writing on subjects of special interest. She and her husband reside in the Antelope Valley just north of Los Angeles. They have three grown children, all happily married with children of their own.

Other Books by Shirley Blackwell Lawrence

Behind Numerology
Numerology and the English Cabalah
The Secret Science of Numerology